WHY FAITH?

"Your Guide to Surviving and Thriving in Tough Times"

By

Dr. A. G. Green

REVISED AND UPDATED VERSION

Copyright © 2009 by Dr. A. G. Green

Why Faith?
"Your Guide to Surviving and Thriving in Tough Times"
by Dr. A. G. Green

Printed in the United States of America

ISBN 978-1-60791-299-6

All rights reserved solely by the author. The author guarantees all contents are original and do not infringe upon the legal rights of any other person or work. No part of this book may be reproduced in any form without the permission of the author. The views expressed in this book are not necessarily those of the publisher.

Unless otherwise indicated, Bible quotations are taken from The King James Version of the Bible, and *The Amplified Bible, Old Testament,* Copyright © 1965, 1987 by the Zondervan Corporation, and *The Amplified Bible New Testament*, Copyright © 1958, 1987 by the Lockman Foundation, La Habra, California, and The Hebrew and Greek words with definitions are taken from Strong, James, The New Strong's Exhaustive Concordance of the Bible, Copyright © 1995 by Thomas Nelson Publishers.

Conventional definitions taken from The Merriam-Webster Dictionary (Paperback) 5th Ed, Springfield, MA: Merriam Webster, Inc., 1994

www.xulonpress.com

DEDICATION

*This Book is dedicated in the memory of four great
women and one great man.
Alberta Green (Grandmother), Uneeda Marshall (Aunt),
Rosie Hardimon (Aunt), Dorothy Walker (Aunt) and
Pastor Eddie Richardson aka "Uncle Ed".*

Thank you, Grandma Green, for exemplifying the true spirit of faith, holiness, and always teaching us the way of the Lord. I think about you often.

Thanks Aunt Uneeda for opening your heart and doors to my siblings and me. Your talks encouraged me to walk by faith and pursue the fullness of God. I can still see your smile and hear your laugh. I miss you terribly. You were a woman of faith.

To Aunt Rosie Hardimon - a.k.a. "Aunt Snookie", thank you for respecting and believing in me. You were one of the meekest and most humble of people that I have ever met.

Aunt Dorothy Walker was one of the sweetest, humble, and most loyal persons that I have ever had the privilege to know. Thank you for being one of the first six members of Rhema Word in Cape Girardeau, Mo. You believed in me and I believed in you. I can't thank you enough for your love and unwavering support.

Uncle Ed, I told you when I last saw you that you were one of my inspirations growing up. I thank you for demonstrating diligence, dedication, and passion for God. Also thanks for letting me preach after church when I was a young boy. I will never forget you.

CONTENTS

Dedication v

Acknowledgements ix

Foreword

Preface xiii

Introduction xv

Chapter 1:   The Author of Faith 17

Chapter 2:   Faith Lost 27

Chapter 3:   Everyone has Faith 37

Chapter 4:   What Abraham Knew 47

Chapter 5:   Faith Is 61

Chapter 6:   Faith Under Fire 71

Chapter 7:   Faith and Patience 83

Chapter 8:   Faith and Hope 95

Chapter 9:   The Faith Power Connection 113

Chapter 10: If at First You Don't Succeed 129

Epilogue 141

Faith Building Tools 143

Notes

ACKNOWLEDGEMENTS

I first want to thank Jehovah-God my savior and redeemer. You are my reason of hope. God I thank you for being everything to me and allowing me to work as one of your representatives in the earth. My existence would be totally meaningless without you. I want to thank my parents whom I love dearly, Bishop Charlie Green Jr. and Evangelist Opal P. Green, for being a living example of Godliness and supporting me along the way. You laid the foundation for my success and I will never forget it. It is my prayer to be able to bless you with whatever you desire.

I want to thank my siblings: Janet (Evangelist and Musician), Charlie III (Pastor and Musician), Andrew (Preacher and Dynamic Vocalist), and Chris (Preacher, Multi-Media Consultant and Resident Comedian). I am your biggest fan and am glad to be your brother. Thank you for all of your support; it means the world to me. To my dear sister-in-law, Tracye Green (deceased but not forgotten), thank you for believing in my ministry; you are one of a kind. To both of my sisters-in-law, Lashonda and Leetha, hang in there; you are special beyond what you know. To my sister-in-law, Shavonna, thank you for investing in me and the ministry; stay connected.

I want to thank my precious grandmother, Illarie Triplett, who is a shining example of what God, willpower, and determination can do. Thanks, Mother, for being strong and helping us when we needed you the most. You are a great source of inspiration for me.

To my uncle, specifically Bishop Nathaniel Green Sr., thanks for always believing in me. Against all odds and opinions you have always been there for me and I will never forget it. To my dear Aunt

Erma, thanks for being a blessing to Vanissa and I. We love you. To all my nieces and nephews I love you.

To my uncles Roy Marshall, Jonathan Green Sr., and Michael Green: Thanks for encouraging me in whatever I set out to do. Your patience, concern and advice have helped me through many challenging times. Uncle Roy, losing Aunt Uneeda wasn't easy. I admire your courage and tenacity in moving forward. Always remember I've got your back! To Uncle Hosea and Aunt Edna Fletcher, thanks for the endless conversations and support. God Bless all of my uncles and aunts.

To my cousins who are like brothers, especially B.A. — Brien Andrews (Musician, Producer, Entrepreneur) of the ATL — my boy — thanks for always being there through thick and thin. You have inspired and encouraged me many times and I appreciate you. Anita Andrews, thanks for your love and kindness it means a lot to me. Thanks to the budding scholar, Terrell Fletcher, who examined the first book and helped me to stay centered. To Myron Fletcher, thank you for all of your support down through the years. To Shonta Green, Anthony D. Green (a.k.a Tony — the other Anthony), Corey Green (a great prophet in the making), Little Joe Green, Greg, Terrance, and all the rest: Thanks for the laughs. God Bless all my cousins. I love you.

To my extended family, Willis B. and Loricestine Green, thanks for supporting me and opening your heart to my family. You don't really know how much you mean to me. (Willis, my brother, passed before this revision. I love you and the next book is in your honor.) To my supportive godnephew and godnieces, I love you.

To Ervin and Gail Ward, thanks for sowing and speaking into my life. We've come a long way since having church in your home. Thank you for all that you do. To Rodney and Helen Baker, I thank God for you and I appreciate your committed support. It's good to know that you have my back. To Tommy and Faye Wells, thanks for your kind words and undying support.

To my longtime friend, Lisa Lane, who has assisted me in so many areas in the ministry and beyond, thank you for your devotion and lending your expertise to many of my endeavors. Your work and loyalty are most appreciated and I thank you for believing in me.

WHY FAITH? *"Your Guide to Surviving and Thriving in Tough Times"*

Thanks to my longtime supporter and friend, Lorenzo Ware. Your optimism is contagious and your words of encouragement have motivated me to reach up.

To my spiritual father Elder Solomon Williams, thanks for imparting into my life and opening the doors of your church when only a few would. Thanks to First Lady Mary Williams; my brother, Terry Williams; my sister, Stacy Williams; my cousins, Crystal and Dwight Johnson; and the New Jerusalem family. Kurt Dunnavant and Calvin Bird, thanks for being good friends. To a spiritual brother like no other, Lamonte Calvin, I appreciate you. To Pastor Earl Grissom and Lady Christine, Pastors Rick and Regina Rogers, Pastor Shonta Green and Lady Dana, and Pastors Thomas and Zsavonda White: Thanks for choosing me as your overseer. It is my pleasure to serve.

To Pastors Gary and Rose Brothers, thanks for looking beyond the natural and into the spiritual. Your insight has prompted you to follow God and open doors for Rhema Word and me. Your genuine, loving spirit is noted and has represented Christ in excellence. Bishop Webb, you are a true friend and confidant thanks for everything. Pastors Johnny and Gladys Hood, thanks for caring. Bishop and Mother William Bird, thanks for listening and showing me kindness.

To Bishop Frank and Jonell Summerfield, thanks for imparting into my life. Bishop, you are one of the greatest teachers and preachers in the world. I am glad to know you. To Pastor Gary and Karen Pleasant, thanks for supporting and believing in me. I thank God for our relationship.

To my precious mother-in-law, Joann McCauley, thank you for always being concerned and doing whatever you could to help. I love you! To my other mother-in-law, Annie McCauley, your sweet spirit is infectious; thanks for accepting me.

To the Rhema Word Breakthrough International Ministries Family, thank you for loving me and supporting me through good times and bad. I thank you for allowing me to be your pastor. You are my heart. Special thanks to my personal assistants, security, and spiritual sons and daughters; it is my pleasure to serve you. Lori Nichols and A. J. Vassar, you are special to me. Never forget your spiritual father always loves you. Betty (Little Betty) Williams, I love you. God bless Jerry and Ramona Stacy. I love you both. To my other mother, Mary Jackson, thanks for your love and support. Thanks to Dorcel and Eric Ware for believing in me.

Last and certainly not least, I want to thank my precious family beginning with my wife Vanissa. We have experienced many things that would have destroyed most relationships, but God brought us through. I want to thank you for being the love of my life and sacrificing yourself to support our family while I pursued full-time ministry. I wouldn't be here today without you. As long as I live it is my priority to serve you. Everything I have is yours and whatever you desire is my responsibility to acquire. I love you more than you could ever know.

I love my precious children: Anthony II, who is sensitive and intelligent, but yet tenacious. And my daughter, Azaryah (Sweetie-pooh), whose intelligence, vivacious zest for life, and quick wit is astounding. Sweetie, you brighten my day.

PREFACE

The purpose of this book is to give some insight into faith and why it is necessary. It is in no way intended to be exhaustive in discussing faith. Nor is it intended to be a manual on the subject. I do believe that it will enlighten people as to the definition, relevance, and necessity of having faith, especially as it relates to believers. I also believe the information shared within this book will empower many people with knowledge concerning faith and enable them to live on a level of faith they have always desired.

More than anything I want people to connect with the heroes or faith-figures of the Bible. The connection I am referring to isn't just limited to their triumphs, but also their failures. I want people to relate to the patriarchs who embraced God. They endured fear, opposition, pain, suffering, imperfection, and persecution without giving up.

We have a human connection to the patriarchs who came before us. And their lives testify that if they can have faith, we can too. Man's capacity of faith and his necessity to possess it cannot be overlooked nor underestimated. I challenge every believer and especially readers of this book to seek God about feeding, nourishing, and using their faith. If you intend to achieve on the highest levels in life and have an intimate relationship with God, you are going to have to possess faith. The journey to accepting and embracing faith begins with an understanding of, *"WHY FAITH?"*

INTRODUCTION

Faith is an intriguing topic to many, especially the Body of Christ. While it is a subject that is discussed heavily, it is still quite misunderstood. I believe that faith is the cornerstone of success for all mankind. To the children of God, it is not merely the lifeline; but the cord that literally connects man to his creator.

The Bible vividly describes the men and women of faith. It blatantly points out the failures and triumphs of humanity in seeking to defy his carnal state and embrace what is invisible. There are glorious accounts of how the heroes of faith gallantly vanquished evil by utilizing faith and achieved supernatural results.

The faith-figures of history (icons or patriarchs of the Bible and secular personalities who are known for living by faith) are presented weekly in churches and other assemblies around the world. Preachers, teachers, motivational speakers, and all who seek to inspire eagerly quote from the lives of faith-figures. It is fascinating to us how people face intimidating and humanly impossible situations; but through faith they triumph.

Movies, television, books, and other media sources constantly share information with the general public about courageous individuals who achieve against all odds. It is a wonderful testament to God, faith, and courage. Many in the daily arena of life seek to pattern their lives after the triumphant masters of faith that they may conquer seemingly insurmountable situations.

It should be noted that although mankind demonstrates an intense appreciation for faith, there is a distinct depreciation occurring simultaneously. Mankind as a whole fails miserably in having faith because of his present state - spiritually, intellectually and emotionally. If many readers of this book were honest, they would admit that they have failed many times in trying to understand faith and live by faith consistently.

Most would rather not have to live by faith. We must admit that faith baffles the senses and defies the very limits of physical reality. The visible and rational are usually more appealing to us than invisible, irrational expectations from an invisible source. We would rather put something in our hands and commence an analytical examination based on visual observation, than to have to deal with nothing.

Be of good cheer. Although faith may be challenging to us, God would not expect it if He knew it would be impossible for man to have it. The key is getting an understanding of *Why Faith?* The Bible answers these crucial questions and unlocks the doors to failure in our attempts to embrace faith. Open your heart and get ready because you are about to operate on a new level of faith.

There are many new features in this revised version that are designed to help your faith to soar. At the end of each chapter you will find Personal Reflections, Intimate Reflections, and the Reflections Journal.

The Personal Reflections contain questions that you can answer either individually or in a small group. The questions are designed to stimulate personal introspection and encourage you to challenge yourself to both change and improve the way you think and live.

The Intimate Reflections are honest, motivational nuggets designed to inspire readers to embrace where they are in life and begin to do the work to see change in their lives.

The Reflections Journal is last. It has been provided for you to answer questions listed in the chapter or just write personal notes about your life. As you are challenged, enlightened, and even empowered, you can record these moments in your journal. Journaling is very cathartic and therapeutic for the mind and body. Enjoy every page of this book and know that your life is about to change for the better.

At the end of the book, look for the Faith Building Tools. These tools are practical instructions on how to increase your faith. If you put these tools to good use, you will see a drastic change in all areas of your life.

Chapter 1

THE AUTHOR OF FAITH

..even God who quickeneth the dead, and calleth those things which be not as though they were. Romans 4:17

To understand the origin of faith is to gain insight into the importance of it and how it relates to the success of all mankind especially the body of Christ. Sometimes knowing where something came from enables us to find easier ways to connect with it. One can work in greater harmony with people if he or she has some knowledge about them. Doctors can usually treat patients better if he knows something about their medical history. We can relate better with dysfunctional people if we know something about their dysfunction and when it began. In a picture, the background sets the stage for the foreground; so it is with faith.

The history of faith can be traced back to God. ***Hebrews 12:2*** says, **"Looking unto Jesus the Author and Finisher of our Faith."** One dictionary defines faith as: *To confide in so as to become without fear; to flee for refuge or to take shelter in; to stay or rest on, to rely on; to believe or take one at his word; to rely upon the promises of another, to put absolute trust in a person without questioning or doubting his faithfulness.* It is evident that God uses faith. He is not only the author and finisher of our belief system of faith, but He also exercises faith in Himself which enables Him to know who He is and what He can do.

"**Even God who quickeneth the dead, and calleth those things which be not as though they were.**" *Romans 4:17.* The God we know as creator and sustainer of all life has always existed. His existence predates that of the planet earth, the universe and all living organisms. He has always been and shall always be. The two English words used in Genesis chapter one which describes the creative exploits of God are the words "created" and "made". The word "created" comes from the Hebrew word *bara. Bara* means to make something from nothing. It is used in *Genesis 1:1*. The word "made" comes from the Hebrew word *asa* which means to make something from something or a material, matter, or substance that already exists. It is used in *Genesis 1:7*.

In *Genesis 1:1* God aggressively creates, without hesitation, something from nothing. He authoritatively calls those things that are not as though they were. He intentionally and purposely extracts, educes or draws out forcibly something from nothing. And in verse three, He gives order and organization to the chaotic. He shows no fear, timidity, or doubt as He goes about His task of creating the world. He knows His assignment and He proceeds with concrete assurance that He has the power to create His vision.

Genesis 1:26 says, **"so let us make man in our image, after our likeness. . ."** *Genesis 1:27* says, **"So God created man in his own image, in the image of God created he him, male and female created he them."** To understand God and his ability to operate in faith is to understand man. Man's likeness of God goes beyond his morality, nature, capacity, and intellectual capabilities. Man has the ability to conjure up thoughts with images and etch it upon the silver screen of his mind. He has the power to produce a pictorial representation of what he imagines. He can then take these images from within and with tangible material give it form and substance. He can literally, forcibly extract something from the invisible and make it visible.

FROM IMAGINATION TO MATERIALIZATION

Have you ever been a part of the process of designing and building a structure? It is amazing and nothing short of phenomenal.

The visionary must envision what type of building he wants to erect. Things like height, shape, contents, features, building materials, etc. must be decided upon. The visionary must see these things in his/her mind first. It is by necessity, desire, or conviction that one attempts to build something. The next step is to share your vision with someone who can capture what you see upon the invisible canvass of your mind and place it on the visible canvass of paper. It usually takes an architect to do this.

The architect not only provides structural drawings which organizes dimensional space, but he/she will also provide an artistic rendering, which is a professional drawing of the finished building that captures the vision as a colorful, living, and bold image. You can actually see something translated or crossover from the realm of imagination to conceptualization on paper. The rendering helps others to see the picture that has always existed on the canvass of your mind. *Faith is reality long before one can see the manifestations of it in the natural.*

The next order of business is to give natural life to the image that has been so wonderfully and accurately depicted on paper. It takes natural substance or visible matter to give form and being to visible things. If you were building a spiritual structure, you would use spiritual material. If you were making a house of glass, then your primary structural material is glass itself. The architect can prescribe the materials needed, but it takes the contractor to physically join the materials together. The contractor literally takes the vision from paper and brings it into a material state where it is touchable. The contractor's trade is to give weight and mass to the vision. He knows just what materials are needed and where they are to be placed in order for your vision to have proper shape and form. He is the master of making abstract things become physical reality.

The process began with the visionary's **imagination** that is then converted by the architect into a sketched **conceptualization** and then transmuted by the contractor into substantial **materialization.** The reality of thought crosses the dimensional plane from the invisible to become substance in the visible realm. The journey of creation begins with the invisible images of the mind, which are then captured on paper and transmuted into physical, concrete, touchable reality.

GOD AND CREATION

Man has received creative abilities from his creator. God saw the world in His mind before He created it. It is a matter of truth that the earth is an inferior model of heaven. Paul says in **Romans 1:20, "For the invisible things of him from the creation of the world are clearly seen, being understood by the things that are made, even his eternal Godhead so that they are without excuse."** I believe that this scripture not only describes natural revelation or God unveiling himself through nature, but that it also gives credence to the invisible things through the visible. One should know through the earth, sun, moon, sky, etc. that God exists. One should also note with other scriptural passages that Heaven exists and many things that the earth possesses Heaven had it first.

The following examples are contents of the New Jerusalem that exists now in Heaven and things that are in Heaven itself *(Revelations 21:2)*. There is a source of **light** *(Revelation 21:23)*. There are **buildings/mansions** *(John 14:1-3)*. There are **streets** *(Revelations 21:21; 22:1-3)*. There are **gates** in heaven *(Revelations 21:12)*. There are **trees** *(Revelations 22:2)*. There are **rivers** *(Revelation 22:1-3)*. There is **water** *(Revelations 7:17)*. There are **animals** *(Revelations 19:11-14)* and many more things in heaven that exist on earth. Earth is an inferior model of Heaven.

In *Genesis 1:3,* it records the beginning of God's verbal commands as He inductively creates. God says, **"Let there be light."** It is evident that from verse two to verse three in Genesis chapter one, we go from the earth being without form and void or chaos and disorder to God establishing order in the earth. *Genesis 1:2* states, **"And darkness was upon the face of the deep."** The earth was completely dark - meaning there was no source of light. In *Genesis 1:3,* God gives permission for light to proceed forth. Where did the light come from? The sun and moon are not created until the fourth day in *Genesis 1:14-19.*

The light of *Genesis 1:3* comes from within God. ***Revelation 21:23*** says, **"And the city had no sun, neither of the moon, to shine in it: for the glory of God did lighten it, and the Lamb is the light thereof."** Heaven has no artificial lighting system. God provides all the light that heaven needs. So as God spoke, **"let there be light"** in Genesis, He gives permission for light to come forth from within Himself and penetrate the darkness that existed on earth.

In creation God moves according to His own vision of purpose. ***Ephesians 1:9*** states, **"Having made known unto us the mystery of his will, according to his good pleasure which he hath purposed in himself."** God willfully premeditated His plan for creation and created according to it. He speaks it and the immaterial becomes material. He speaks and the mysterious is made plain. He speaks and does so, knowing with full assurance that He is all-powerful. Even today He is yet calling things into existence in the lives of human beings. He alone can speak something into your life where there literally was nothing.

GOD IS THE GREATEST GUARANTOR OF ANY COVENANT

Our God exercises faith in Himself. In taking an oath to affirm and ensure the covenant between Himself and man, God swore by Himself.

> **"And said, by myself have I sworn, saith the LORD, for because thou hast done this thing, and hast not withheld thy son, thine only son."** *Genesis 22:16*

> **"For when God made promise to Abraham, because he could swear by no greater, he sware by himself."** *Hebrews 6:13*

When parties enter into covenant, they must be assured that each shall keep his oath. The strength of the covenant is determined by the parties who committed themselves to it. The covenant is only as good as a person's word and unless provisions are in the covenant to exceed the life span of those who made the agreement, it usually dies with them. Let's say that you made a covenant with a neighbor that stated that each one could enter on the other's personal property and freely use whatever was available on it. In order for this covenant to be effective, it must be supported by certain factors:

(1) The persons who make the covenant must be truthful and trustworthy. If a person can't be trusted, then there is no certainty that the covenant will be honored.

(2) There must be a token or evidence that serves as proof that the covenant has been made. It could be blood that was shed to ratify the covenant leaving a scar on the participants as evidence; or it could be a piece of paper with signatures that validates the covenant. God made a covenant with Noah and man to never destroy the world again by water. The proof of the covenant was the rainbow in the sky. The rainbow serves as a reminder to man in every generation that God would never use water to destroy the earth again.

(3) The covenant is only as good as the existence of the person. When people enter into covenant, they can only abide by it if they are alive. If provisions are not made for the covenant to be handed down and honored from generation to generation, it will stop with the death of the ones who made the covenant.

If Bill and John entered into a covenant of being able to access each other's property freely and use whatever was located on it, the strength of the covenant hinges upon the existence of the covenant makers. Even if the covenant includes a generational clause, there is no guarantee that the survivors will adhere to it. The only way to be certain that the covenant will be kept is that those who made it must be alive to keep it.

The eagerness of God to swear by Himself proves that He has faith in Himself. Who better to keep a covenant than the One who is omnipotent, omniscient, immutable, and everlasting? The scripture declares, "**Know therefore that the Lord thy God, he is God, the faithful God, which keepeth covenant and mercy with them that love him and keep his commandments to a thousand generations.**" *Deuteronomy 7:9*

God exercises faith in Himself and we are to have faith in Him. A thousand generations emphasizes the unlimited commitment of God to His people.

God has assured us through creation and declaring Himself as the guarantor in making covenants with man that He is the indisputable embodiment of faith. *It takes faith to stare into the emptiness of nothing and declare the fullness of something.* It takes faith and love to enter into covenant with man knowing that his frailty will prohibit him from keeping any covenant eternally. Undeterred by this weakness, God still uses Himself as guarantor to ensure the covenant will remain in effect for those who obey Him. God's faith knows no limits. His faith stems from the intrinsic sovereignty of His supreme authority that transcends the comprehensibility of all mankind and defies all space and time.

As a guarantor, God impeccably fits every requirement to uphold and honor any covenant.

1) **<u>He is trustworthy.</u> "God is not a man, that he should lie; neither the son of man, that he should repent: hath he said, and shall he not do it? or hath he spoken, and shall he not make it good?"** *Numbers 23:19*
2) **<u>He has provided the proof or token that the covenant was ratified through the life, death, burial, and resurrection of Jesus who then released salvation through the Holy Spirit. Now when we receive Christ into our hearts as Lord and Savior, the Spirit bears witness.</u> "14) How much more shall the blood of Christ, who through the eternal Spirit offered himself without spot to God, purge your conscience from dead works to serve the living God? 15) And for this cause he is the mediator of the new testament, that by means of death, for the redemption of the transgressions that were under the first testament, they which are called might receive the promise of eternal inheritance. 16) For where a testament is, there must also of necessity be the death of the testator. 17) For a testament is of force after men are dead: otherwise it is of no strength at all while the testator liveth."** *Hebrews 9:14-17*

> **The Spirit itself beareth witness with our spirit that we are the children of God.** *Romans 8:16*
> 3) <u>**His existence is eternal; so the covenant he makes with us is guaranteed forever.**</u> **"The eternal God is thy refuge and underneath are the everlasting arms: and he shall thrust out the enemy from before thee; and shall say, Destroy them."** *Deuteronomy 33:27*

"Now unto the King eternal, immortal, invisible, the only wise God, be honour and glory for ever and ever. Amen." *1 Timothy 1:17*

The Author of faith exercises faith. And man, who was created in the image of God, partakes of the likeness of God and therefore, has the ability to exercise faith in God and apply it wherever he chooses. If man wants to master faith and learn how to use it daily, he must seek wisdom from the author of faith which is the true and living God.

PERSONAL REFLECTIONS

Please feel free to discuss these questions with friends, family, or a small group. Search yourself with an open heart and let God fill your every need and desire.

1. How do Hebrews 12:2 and Romans 4:17 relate to God and faith?
2. Under the subheading "From Imagination to Materialization", the author describes the process that a visionary takes to bring something into existence. Can you relate to this? Have you ever had to plan, plot, build, or organize something?
3. Can you see how you have received creative abilities from God?
4. What are the three requirements for covenant that the author mentions?
5. How does God's faith affect His covenant relationship with us?
6. Are you in covenant with anyone? If so, are they trustworthy?

INTIMATE REFLECTIONS

God is the Author and Creator of our faith. He operates by utilizing faith within Himself. We must learn how to embrace our Creator and draw closer to Him in intimacy. His love beckons us to come and fall into His eternal arms. He will teach us how to love and operate in faith beyond our present limitations. Believers should expect covenant ties with God to bring joy and fullness to their lives. Unbelievers are welcome to embrace the eternal well spring that flows from God that quenches every desire and empowers every dream. You don't have to understand Him fully; just trust Him and your life will never be the same.

WHY FAITH? "Your Guide to Surviving and Thriving in Tough Times"

REFLECTIONS JOURNAL

Chapter 2

FAITH LOST

... she took of the fruit thereof and did eat and gave also to her husband with her and he did eat. Genesis 3:6b

Imagine a world with no pollution, a sky as transparent as clear glass, the sun's rays penetrate the atmosphere enabling one to see with perfect clarity for miles, and behold the wonder of God's creation. Animals live together in perfect unity. Lions and lambs stand side by side without a tinge of uneasiness. There is a perfect blending of peace and harmony across the landscape of all creation. Man honors the land and the land yields endless productivity. Man rules without the threat of war and the need of any bloodshed. All creation sings with a melody of praise paying homage to the one who gave to all life and being. The creator fellowships with the creature in love, trust, honor, and reverence.

The world I am speaking of doesn't have sickness, poverty, politics, hate, greed, religion, jealousy, or sin. The goodness of creation exists in super-abundance. Time is not a factor in this world. There is no such thing as age or growing old.

FAITH IN THE GARDEN

In listening to the utopia-like description, someone's first thought might be heaven, but actually I was describing the earth in Adam and Eve's generation. Their central headquarters was the Garden of Eden, but God gave man dominion over the whole earth. The earth existed in a steady state of balance - biologically, ecologically, and spiritually. Adam and Eve wanted for nothing. God provided every thing they needed and could possibly want. We don't know how long they ruled the earth from the Garden of Eden before they sinned, but it appears that for a time they had faith in God and His word. **"And the Lord God commanded the man saying, of every tree of the garden thou mayest freely eat. But of the tree of knowledge of good and evil thou shalt not eat of it, for in the day that thou eatest thereof thou shalt surely die."** *Genesis 2:16-17*

We don't know when God gave the commandment or how long it took Adam and Eve to violate it; but it seems as if they abided by it for a fair amount of time. God presented a test to his children. If man could be trusted with his freewill and not use it to disobey God, he could be trusted to live forever. The result of his disobedience would cost him almost everything including his intimacy with God. In order to keep the commandment, they had to have faith in what God said.

EVE'S FAITH WAS CHALLENGED

Listen to Eve's conversation with the serpent, **"And the woman said unto the serpent we may eat of the fruit of the trees of the garden. But of the fruit of the tree which is in the midst of the garden, God hath said, Ye shall not eat of it neither shall ye touch it lest ye die."** *Genesis 3:2-3* It is apparent that Eve misquoted God by saying, "neither shall ye touch it," but her dialogue with the serpent proves that she walked in obedience for a time.

Let us not forget how this conversation started. The serpent approached Eve, **"he said unto the woman yea hath God said ye shall not eat of every tree of the garden?"** *Genesis 3:1b* Satan, utilizing the body of a serpent, intentionally twists up what God says to strike up a conversation with Eve. The Amplified Bible says it like this, **"And he [Satan] said to the woman, can it really be that God has said, you shall not eat from every tree of the garden?"**

Satan intentionally distorts what God has said. His distortion is enough to draw Eve into a conversation.

I know that most of you are familiar with the three avenues of temptation: *the lust of the flesh, the lust of the eyes,* and *the pride of life.* In knowing this, I don't want you to overlook the fact that Satan first wants to test the believer to see just what they know. Can you quote the word of God for your life correctly or are you walking in error? Eve's answer to Satan was an indication that:

1) **She wasn't completely sure of what God really said.**
2) **By adding that she couldn't touch, it indicated that consciously she desired to at least be able to touch the fruit, if not eat it.**
3) **Her exchange of conversation concerning the fruit opened a door for Satan to corrupt her thinking with his power of suggestion and persuasion.**

If you remember, Satan tried a similar ploy on Christ by misquoting the word of God. Jesus, who was the Word, knew the word and answered Satan with the word. Jesus resisted Satan's advances with the word of God. His responses and resistance to Satan proved to the enemy that Jesus knew the word and could not be bought, sold, or deceived. Jesus refused to carry on a lengthy conversation with Satan. He rebuked him and went on his way. (Matthews 4:1-11)

Satan intends to wear us down with unending, morbid, negative words about our lives. He speaks contrary to God's will for our lives. If you give him an ear, he will eventually corrupt your thinking and cause you to reevaluate God's will for your life. Eve moved in her thinking from the truth of knowing not to eat the fruit to actually eating it and recruiting her husband to join her.

Satan had already appealed to her eyes and flesh. Now he appeals to her pride by saying, **"ye shall not surely die. For God doth know that in the day ye eat thereof, then your eyes shall be opened and ye shall be as gods knowing good and evil."** *Genesis 3:2-3* Satan's final blow has been rendered. He literally calls God a liar and Eve lost her faith in God and his word by eating the fruit.

When it is all said and done, the final analysis of every trial, tribulation, and attack from the enemy is simply Satan saying God is a liar. What God said you can have, you can't. What God said he would do, he won't. He boldly suggests to us, "Do not believe whatever God says." It is not that Satan doesn't believe God. He actually is familiar with God's power and truthfulness, but his objective is to convince you that God cannot be trusted. The erosion of faith in the human race began with Eve, but it officially took hold and was sealed when Adam, the head of the human race, ate the fruit.

"And the woman saw that the tree was good for food, and that it was pleasant to the eyes, and a tree to be desired to make one wise, she took of the fruit thereof, and did eat, and gave also unto her husband with her, and he did eat. And the eyes of them both were opened, and they knew that they were naked and they sewed fig leaves together and made themselves aprons." *Genesis 3:6-7* Adam, as the head, was entrusted with the commandment. And when he partook of the fruit, the very nature of man was changed. (1Timothy 2:14)

After the fall of Adam, man now has a nature that innately doubts God and gravitates toward evil. (Psalm 51:5) Man finds himself in a dilemma where he has a propensity to sin and is inclined in his ways to follow the path of evil. The Apostle Paul says, **"But I see another law in my members, warring against the law of my mind, and bringing me into captivity to the law of sin which is in my members."** *Romans 7:23*

THE BATTLE OF FLESH VERSUS THE SPIRIT RAGES DAILY

Paul's epic struggles of flesh against spirit, sin against righteousness, and good versus evil are displayed in the preceding text. Adam's sin released a battle of good versus evil within man that only God could remedy. The battle of the mind versus the spirit is a daily struggle. The body of Christ and especially Christian leadership has masked the daily struggle of good and evil within. We speak so often of striving for perfection and holiness which are both necessary teachings, but we fail to be transparent in allowing people to know that every human being experiences the same challenges of fighting to do what is right. Paul sums it up using the term "warring". This describes a war against or the opposing of his mind.

The sin nature is in direct contradiction to God. We must understand that there is an innate thrust to disobey God and his word. We must all deal with the enemy within. There are days where some struggle to attend church and others struggle to stay faithful to the marriage vow. Some struggle just to say the right things or treat people right when they have been done wrong. Some struggle in believing God. Some struggle with lust, greed, lying, stealing, cheating, dishonesty, bad attitudes, idolatry, family idolatry, etc. Some struggle with worldliness, impure thoughts, insecurity, depression, etc.

I could tell you about the various struggles of men and women in the body of Christ that I know about personally. Some names you would recognize and others you wouldn't. Their struggles range from sexual promiscuity to alcoholism to homosexuality. It is never acceptable to justify sin, but Christianity must do a better job of painting a real picture of human nature that is tainted by sin and how to deal with it. **We all struggle with something. The question is not If, but what.**

In all of our struggles, it seems as if sin always attacks our faith in God and ourselves.

Sin and faith in God are diametrically opposed. Man's fallen nature is corrupt and intends to follow sin's lusts. Sin has an agenda that doesn't include following God. Sin is rebellion against God. Sin thinks, acts, works, and worships independently of God. Sin has completely mangled and dismantled the spiritual and moral compass of man. Man remains blind in the face of impending destruction.

As a youngster, I tried many strange things. One, in particular, was walking blindly. I have always had a peculiar curiosity with things I hadn't yet experienced. I often wondered what it felt like to be blind. I remember closing my eyes and trying to find my way throughout the house. I even remember cutting all the lights off in the room to create a situation where not even a pinhead of light penetrated. I then tried to find my way through this maze of darkness. My room literally became unknown to me. Inevitably I bumped my knee, stubbed my toe, stumbled over objects, and clumsily felt my way through the groping darkness. I could never manage to exit the room without making contact with something. My points of reference to aid me in this quest were the walls, furniture, and other large objects.

In all of my attempts, I could never master walking in the dark or navigating effectively with my eyes closed. In the dark, I was completely out of my zone of normality. My eyes were useless because no light could penetrate the barrier of curtains and window blinds; so I struggled in a place I otherwise was familiar with. The flip of a switch changed the atmosphere from light to darkness completely neutralizing the senses, particularly my eyes, and temporarily crippled me.

ADAM'S SIN

When Adam sinned, the whole human race which was genetically and spiritually contained within his loins was stricken with corruption and spiritual blindness. Sin cast a veil upon the face of the human race and dimmed the light in Adam's spirit. It was with one act of sin that the switch was flipped from light to darkness. Man's experience with God now is hazy and cloudy. What man now sees doesn't resemble what Adam and Eve saw before they disobeyed. **"For now we see through a glass, darkly; but then face to face now I know in part but then shall I know even as also I am known."** *1 Corinthians 13:12*

Darkness entered into the human experience disturbing the three dimensional balance within man. Man, who is really a spirit, is out of touch with spiritual realities. The mind, will, emotions, and base, fleshly desires rule mankind. Man's sense knowledge decodes, deciphers, and interprets his reality for him. The fall of Adam has caused mankind to become a prisoner of the visible. Man is generally ignorant of things outside the discernable scope of his organically comprised sense organs. Spiritually, he is dead unless given life through Jesus Christ. (Ephesians 2:1) His spiritual death is the basis of his disconnection from the true reality of whom he was created to be and who his creator is. The loss of faith has marred man's view of God and his purpose.

Man was once a creature who walked in the light of understanding without a veil covering his eyes and mind. He viewed God with transparency and clarity; but when sin entered into the human race with the submission of Adam to the temptation of Satan, man not only lost his way, he lost his faith.

PERSONAL REFLECTIONS

Please feel free to discuss these questions with friends, family or a small group. Search yourself with an open heart and let God fill your every need and desire.

1. What was the commandment that God gave Adam and Eve in the garden?
2. Has God ever commanded you to do something?
3. What are the three avenues of temptation?
4. What is your biggest temptation? How are you dealing with it?
5. Eve's conversation with the serpent indicates what?
6. Was Eve really prepared to defend herself against the serpent? Are you prepared to defend yourself against your enemies?
7. When it is all said and done, the final analysis of every trial, tribulation, and attack from the enemy is simply Satan saying God is a liar. What things have God told you that Satan has tried to make you think is a lie?
8. Describe the battle of the flesh versus the spirit in your personal life and explain how Adam's sin has affected your struggle? Are you winning or losing the struggle?

INTIMATE REFLECTIONS

Many of us can relate to Eve. She literally had whatever her heart desired. She had a good husband, great job, and all the luxuries afforded to any wealthy person. Why did she eat of the fruit and convince her husband to follow her example? Simply stated, she was tempted and enticed. Sometimes our lust for more can hinder our relationship with God. We must learn how to rest in what he has already provided and wait patiently for what is to come. Remember Eve as you go about your day and don't make the same mistake she did. Stay away from things that God has said are forbidden and be thankful for what He says is allowable. Some doors are better shut and some gifts are better to be refused.

REFLECTIONS JOURNAL

Chapter 3

EVERYONE HAS FAITH

..God hath dealt to every man the measure of faith.
Romans 12:3b

God has provided all of his creation, spiritual and natural alike, with everything they need to survive and thrive. Healthy infants are equipped from birth with everything they need to survive. The various biological systems we are born with, although they are new at birth, yet function with precision and advance with age. An infant girl is born with two million eggs which will last her a lifetime. Male and Female babies are born with billions of brain cells that are designed to last for the duration of life. The physical body of the human race is well stocked and equipped to handle the cycles of growth and maturity that lay ahead.

It is amazing how God created Adam and Eve as fully, functional adults. They were instantly capable of performing complex functions intellectually, psychologically, and physically. God created them whole and complete. Adam and Eve contained pure strands of DNA void of defects or imperfections. When Adam fell, sin began to contaminate the gene pool; but man is yet a remarkable creature. Adam and Eve were created as adults, but since them, everyone has been born in reverse as infants who yet have the potentiality at birth to evolve to adulthood.

When we consider the body, we usually base what we consider to be normal on the standards of normality the human race has adopted for itself. For example, it is considered normal to be born with two eyes, two ears, two legs, etc. If someone is missing one of these things, then that person is considered to have some abnormalities. There are some things that every human being must have to survive. While we have taken inventory physically, we have failed to acknowledge the intangible things that every human being must have to survive and to experience any measure of success.

What is it that makes nerdy, endomorphic children become giant, mature business tycoons? What is it that transforms a lanky teenager to a brass, strapping, confident, and dominant athlete? What is the driving force that enables you to go through intimidating situations without prior experience and end up on top? It wasn't just your intellect, wisdom, chance, or timing. All these are key factors. But the one thing that connects all of them together is faith.

Many believe that faith is just for the righteous, excluding the natural man altogether. Man is a three dimensional being - spirit, soul, and body. (1 Thessalonians 5:23) The real essence of man is his spirit and soul which are both immaterial substances that make up his core. The tri-unity of man is three substances in one.

While it is important to acknowledge the three dimensional parts of man, we must not lose sight that they are interconnected and function as one compact unit.

THE REALM OF FLESH AND SPIRIT

The natural man, prior to conversion, is yet able to access the spiritual universe because he is a spirit. The basic elemental composition of things in the spirit realm is homogeneous in substance with all spiritual matter whether it is spiritual buildings or spiritual beings. The spirit is thereby subject to the laws that govern the spiritual universe. The same principles apply for the physical dimension that consists of physical matter with physical laws that govern the physical realm.

All physical matter from microscopic particles of the atom to the visible concrete superstructures of skyscrapers exists on the same dimensional plane and is subject to the limitations of the physical universe. The limitations of the physical are imposed on all physical matter. Physics teaches us that mass is the amount of matter in an object and weight is the pull of gravity on a given mass. The Law of Gravity basically says that what goes up must come down. These aforementioned laws apply to objects in the physical realm regardless of its shape or size.

Since man fell, he has been dominated by his carnal mind and flesh. The carnal mind is directly influenced by the flesh or senses. Man is driven by his intellect, emotions, and sensuality. As a result he tends to focus more on his self-consciousness and world-consciousness than his God-consciousness. He concentrates on seeing and understanding through the physical organ of the human brain and not the spiritual man. The human brain certainly has an important function and without it, we couldn't operate in the physical universe but our true essence of being is as a spirit. Due to carnal mindsets and sensual dominance, man acknowledges confidence but doesn't quite understand that many times he is really using human faith.

Human faith allows us to have confidence in our own natural abilities and accomplish what we attempt to with our talents. When I think of talents, I think of the natural endowments a person has. There are many things we are talented to do that are not listed as a gift of the spirit in the Bible; but they are definitely talents. We have talented artists, geniuses, athletes, etc.; but these are not spiritual gifts. While talents are natural abilities, God does anoint the natural with the spirit or supernatural. ***1Kings 18:41-46*** records how Elijah ran for almost thirty miles in front of Ahab and his chariot of horses. Running is a natural, physical ability of man; but when the spirit anoints the natural, supernatural feats can be accomplished to the glory of God.

FAITH

Human faith enables us to effectively utilize the natural abilities and talents we have which enables us to achieve a task successfully. Many self-help books or motivational seminars appeal to our natural abilities of the mind and its vast potentiality to build our confidence to utilize our talents to the optimal capacity. While the human mind has untapped wells of potential and is incredibly potent when utilized as God intended. The untold, phenomenal capabilities of the human mind shouldn't be mistaken for spiritual power. The powers of the human mind and powers of the spirit aren't the same.

Having said all of that, you may not think, feel, or act like it; but you have faith. You have faith to engage natural talents and you have faith to engage spiritual gifts. It takes faith to operate in the gifts of the Spirit. ***Romans 12:6*** **"Having then gifts differing according to the grace that is given to us, whether prophecy let us prophesy according to the proportion of faith."** The second part of the verse says, **"whether prophecy let us prophesy according to the proportion of faith."** When we prophesy, we do so by faith believing and knowing that we can hear from God and while in the midst of prophesying, are hearing from Him. The ability to see into the future is inspired by a supernatural, spiritual Source.

It takes faith to receive from an invisible, spiritual source. Our whole relationship with God, from salvation to the preaching of the Gospel, is based upon faith. It is difficult for people to hear from God when their faith is shaky. ***James 1:6-7,*** **"But let him ask in faith nothing wavering. For he that wavereth is like a wave of the sea driven with the wind and tossed. For let not that man think that he shall receive anything of the Lord."** James candidly says if you are wavering in your faith, don't think that you are going to receive anything from the Lord. If one is to operate in the gifts or function in a ministry office, they must have faith.

I remember while on the field as a full-time evangelist prior to pastoring, I encountered a situation where I publicly shared a word from God with a prominent member of the church. Since the Lord started using me to share prophetically and through a word of wisdom and knowledge years ago, he has given me uncanny accuracy in speaking with pinpointed precision into the lives of many. That is not to say that I haven't ever missed God; but I have grown to know His voice. And the fruit is that what He gives me to speak to others eventually proves to be true.

Well on this particular occasion, the person I was ministering to publicly rejected what I said stating that I was wrong. I was stunned.

I apologized and even tried to justify what I said, but the damage had been done. I was publicly humiliated and to some the validity of my ministry came into question. I became the subject of conversation publicly and privately. My faith to operate in the spiritual gifts and prophesy was deeply affected. It caused me to question God and myself.

Although that has been many years ago and I have ministered to many people since then and have shared specific things that only God could reveal, I yet sometimes feel I lost something that day which hasn't been restored. The thing that consoles me is that even to this day, I yet meet countless people whom I don't know personally but they were in attendance that day and they all tell me that everything I said was true.

EVERYONE HAS FAITH

Faith is not just for the privileged or a select group of people. Some believe that only preachers, teachers, missionaries, experienced saints, and God's favorites have faith. Is that what the Bible says? Let's examine the scripture, **"For I say to the grace given unto me, to every man that is among you, not to think of himself more highly than he ought to think, but to think soberly, according as God hath dealt to every man the measure of faith."** *Romans 12:3*

The Amplified Bible says, **"For by the grace (unmerited favor of God) given to me I warn everyone among you not to estimate and think of himself more highly than he ought [not to have an exaggerated opinion of his own importance], but to rate his ability with sober judgment, each according to the degree of faith apportioned by God to him."**

In ***Romans 12:3b,*** the first part of the verse encourages man not to exaggerate or overrate his own importance. Paul wants to remind us that we are nothing without God. Many have arrogantly and others innocently overrated their faith. Your ability to receive from God is largely predicated on your faith. This is not to say that God is limited to work only within the confines of faith. The Bible records on many occasions that Jesus had compassion and healed them. His compassion didn't recognize faith, but His heart was moved to heal them and because He could, He did.

The Sovereignty of God is unlimited. There are times God chooses to do for us simply because we belong to Him. Man esteems himself through pride, ignorance, zeal, greed, etc. He quickly finds out that as a general rule with God, you have to believe and then you will receive. Believers and unbelievers are still required of God to exercise faith daily.

In making the transition to the second half of the verse, he wants you to measure or qualify yourself according to the portion of faith that God has given you. Let's look at the text more closely. **"God hath dealt to every man the measure of faith."** God *(theos)* - the supreme deity analogous with a magistrate authority - hath **dealt** *(merizo)* - apportion, bestow, share - with every man the **measure** *(metron)* - a limited portion - of **faith** *(pistis)* - a credence, conviction of religious truth of God.

Every man or woman has enough faith to embrace God. *God, the Supreme Being, has dealt or bestowed to every man the measure, or a limited portion of faith, a conviction of truth about God.* God has equipped all mankind with faith and the ability to develop it.

We need to abandon our flawed self-analysis that says God has left us out. When things aren't going like we desire or when trouble seems to have made a home in our personal lives, it is tempting to think God has overlooked us.

If most people would be honest, they have felt like this at some time or another in their lives. I vividly remember during the very lean years of my life when I was an unknown full-time evangelist wondering if I were left out. I had a fledgling evangelistic ministry that was birthed out of a call from God and yet I was barely surviving. I had a family to support, but yet I obeyed God and gave up a job working for a Fortune 500 Company that not only paid well, but also offered me a future abounding with great potential. I stepped out by faith obeying God and soon became well acquainted with suffering. I knew I was committed. I sought God daily. I kept myself in His presence and did what I could in seeking out engagements and I still fell short.

The price I paid was higher than most will ever know. My marriage was in critical condition and our finances were at rock bottom. I recall one incident where my son, who was just a baby at the time, needed diapers. Here I am: A man of God preaching faith, conducting revivals, prophesying, and speaking into the lives of many; but I couldn't even afford to buy a package of diapers for my baby. I wept profusely staining my clothes with tears of humility and moistening my face with the seasoning of salty tears. What kind of man was I? Where was God? I felt as if God had abandoned me. That same night God touched the heart of an uncle who came by and gave us enough money to buy pampers and food. Again, God proved that He was with me.

GOD HAS NOT FORGOTTEN YOU

We must know that even when it comes to faith, God has not forsaken us. He has equipped us with enough faith to embrace Him. Biblical and world history proves that man has always embraced God through faith. Mankind, wherever he has existed whether in a civilized society or in the brush of an undeveloped country, has an innate longing to embrace God. It is unnatural for man to reject the truth of a divine creator. *Psalms 53:1,* **"The fool hath said in his heart, there is no God corrupt are they and have done abominable iniquity, there is none that doeth good."** The word "fool" comes from the Hebrew word *nabal* which means a stupid, wicked, vile person.

It is stupidity, wickedness, and vileness that would cause a person to say there is no God. As the verse continues, it states they are corrupt. Man, in his many attempts, has failed by worshiping God as an element of nature such as wind, rain, fire, or the earth. He has even erected images to worship, but this is all driven by an inner craving and an intangible faith to relate to his God. We have been designed to operate by faith and connect to God with it. While some in the scientific and psychological communities have attempted to convince man through material, empirical evidence that God doesn't exist, the Bible emphatically acknowledges His existence and glaringly declares no matter who you are that if you reject the very existence of God, you are a fool.

Among the many misconceptions about faith that exists is that you must have the faith of Abraham, Moses, or some other known faith-figure of the Bible to succeed and receive from God. The Bible records in ***Matthew 17:20,*** **"And Jesus said unto them, because of your unbelief, for verily I say unto you, If ye have faith as a grain of mustard seed, ye shall say unto this mountain, remove hence to yonder place, and it shall remove and nothing shall be impossible unto you."** Most know about the miniature size of a mustard seed and the transformation from a seed to a towering tree, but many miss the second most significant message that is overlooked within this verse. *That message is that you don't need great faith to get results. Frankly, most people will never have it!*

We should strive to feed our faith so that it will grow. However, God understands man's struggles against the carnal mind, evil spirits, and world system. As a result, many will only embrace God with less than great faith. If you have read the Gospels, you will see that Jesus was overjoyed whenever He met someone who demonstrated great faith. He reacted this way because many people He met, including His disciples, had little or weak faith. If you talk to people, you will soon find out that great faith in God is rare these days. Many have more faith in themselves, denominations, doctrines, and men than in God.

You were born with limbs, organs, and other necessary organic material necessary to survive in the natural realm. You were also given a measure of faith to ensure your survival in both the natural and spiritual realm. I want you to be encouraged to know that whatever your status — social, economic, spiritual, ethnic, etc., God has given you a measure of faith. And even a small portion, when used, will bring great results.

WHY FAITH? *"Your Guide to Surviving and Thriving in Tough Times"*

PERSONAL REFLECTIONS

Please feel free to discuss these questions with friends, family or a small group. Search yourself with an open heart and let God fill your every need and desire.

1. According to 1 Thessalonians 5:23, what is man?
2. Since man fell, he has been dominated by what?
3. What is human faith? What does it help us do?
4. What are talents and spiritual gifts? What is the difference?
5. List any talents you may have? Are you using them? If not, why?
6. List any spiritual gifts you may have? Are you using them? If not, why?
7. How do Romans 12:3 apply to you? Are you using your faith? If so, how?

INTIMATE REFLECTIONS

For those who have an understanding of spiritual things, it is common knowledge that man is dominated by his carnal, fleshly, worldly, self-absorbed mind. Our daily battle is to walk in the spiritual. One critical key to living a fulfilling life is to utilize our natural and spiritual talents. Every human being comes equipped with some kind of natural talent and spiritual gift. What do you like to do? What is your passion? What are you known for being critical of? Your interest, quirks, or passion could very well be what you are talented or gifted in doing. Seek God for understanding as it relates to what talents or gifts He has endowed you with. A person who finds their niche in life finds happiness. Unhappy people generally have an identity crisis; they don't know who or what they should be doing. People who are utilizing their talents and gifts tend to be happier people. Are you happy? Trust God with what He has given you. Use your talents and gifts to help many people and He will ensure that you prosper.

WHY FAITH? "Your Guide to Surviving and Thriving in Tough Times"

REFLECTIONS JOURNAL

Chapter 4

WHAT ABRAHAM KNEW

..so Abram departed as the Lord had spoken unto him.
Genesis 12:4a

ALL OF GOD'S SERVANTS HAD TO USE FAITH

It is difficult to discuss the subject of faith as it pertains to God and His people without mentioning Abraham. Abraham is respected and hailed throughout the world. He is mentioned favorably by the three major religions of the world. My recollection of Abraham doesn't recall him as a flawless man who was always as solid as a rock. Abraham had his share of struggles like most, but something separated him from the rest of the pack.

While I am at this station, we must be careful not to deify or mystify people. The Bible is a record of history that reveals God to Man. God is the unlimited deity and man is the limited being. The Bible is clear on the point of man's mortality and God's eternality. We should not elevate the faith figures of the Bible beyond humanity. Our elevation of Biblical characters creates a chasm between them and us. Many have placed them in a category that is beyond human and unknowingly diminish themselves along with the power of God's Word for us.

The Bible is not about perfect people nor is it written to perfect people. Our failure to identify with the patriarchs on a human level distorts our ability to believe that Gods' Word will work for us. The body of Christ must know that as a human being no Biblical personality was somehow better and more deserving than us. To subscribe to such a belief would consciously and unconsciously disqualify us from being able to wholly receive the promises of God. For example, some would say Moses was the great deliverer and God revealed Himself to him because he was special. They would then say Moses was greater than most men; therefore we shouldn't expect to have the same kind of relationship with God.

Truthfully, God is not speaking to most people face to face like He did Moses, but many have had glorious encounters with God that were similar. **"The secret of the Lord is with them that fear him and he will show them his covenant."** *Psalm 25:14* If you seek the Lord, He will reveal Himself to you in a special way. Moses is not the only one to whom God has revealed Himself.

We should know that Moses was not exempt. He had to use faith just like us in order to see the supernatural manifested. Don't disqualify yourself by saying, "I'm not Moses, Abraham, David, etc."

Paul and Barnabas, after working a miracle, began to be worshipped by men. They hastily corrected the crowd by identifying themselves as men and not gods. (Acts 14:11-15) There has been a lot said about Abraham. Books have been devoted to him, preachers have devoted untold hours to proclaiming his plight, and unacknowledged billions have been inspired throughout time by his example. I believe that the early record of God speaking to Abraham in *Genesis 12:1-4* quickly summarizes the type of man he was.

ABRAHAM'S SIMPLE FORMULA

"So Abram departed as the Lord had spoken unto him and Lot went with him and Abram was seventy and five years old when he departed out of Haran." *Genesis 12:4.* The first part of the verse states, **"Abram departed as the Lord had spoken unto him."** It appears from reading *Genesis 11:31* that Abram had been spoken to before by God because his father appeared to be moving with him but died on the way to Canaan. Abram impresses me because he buries his father and continues his journey.

It is a fact that you can't take everyone with you on the journey of faith. Those who accompany you and succumb to death, unbelief, or simply become a burden should be buried. Abraham had a funeral, mourned his father's death, buried him, and kept moving. When God speaks and you follow Him, be prepared to bury people close to you along the way. Everybody that starts with you won't finish with you. Appreciate them for their contributions, mourn their loss, bury them, and then move forward and don't look back.

Isn't it amazing how many books have been written about faith? Authors have dissected and surgically explored the body of faith in an attempt to understand it and simplify it for the masses. Many have written about how to get, utilize, build, and even use faith. I have read many such books and was enlightened but the question I want to ask is what did Abraham really do? Before God put Abraham in a deep sleep and made a covenant with him in terms and deeds he could understand, what did Abraham really do? (Genesis 15:12-18) What did he do before God reminded him of his covenant word? I'll tell you what the Bible states he did. It says, **"Abram departed as the Lord had spoken unto him."**

You don't have to jump through hoops. You don't have to hear a thousand sermons. You don't have to be saved 20 years. You don't have to have a title or position in the church. You don't have to have a testimony of once being half dead because of sickness, gang banging, or severe drug addiction. These things are not a requirement to have faith. *Abraham simply did what God told him to do!*

The Bible states, **"Abram departed as the Lord had spoken unto him."** In other words, God spoke and Abraham obeyed. Somebody may say, "No, preacher, there must be more to it than that." Yes, you're right. There is more afterwards, but not before. ***The manifestations of faith are not revealed before, but afterwards***. Abraham did not receive Isaac before faith, but afterwards. Israel did not receive the promised land before faith, but afterwards. We do not receive salvation before faith, but afterwards. ***Faith must first be deployed and then the manifestations of it will be revealed.*** Abram did what God said. How often have we argued with God?

How often do we struggle with something because we don't want to do it? How often do we withdraw from God's Word for us because we don't understand? How often do we fear what we can't see? We have grown accustomed to living our lives by shear, practical, logical intellect. It is our intellect and carnal mind that usually convinces us that the unseen and unknown are baseless. Mankind has become sense-ruled and therefore enslaved to a sense-perceived reality.

Abraham didn't have sensible information or a database to draw from. He only had his faith. He only had faith in what God had spoken unto him. He had faith before God confirmed Himself. His faith started before he left his land of nativity. He strictly responded to the call and believed in the One who called him. ***He knew God was worthy of his faith.*** Abraham's itinerary took him into the caverns of human frailty along the meandering streams of doubt and eventually to the prolific prodigious plains of the Promised Land. His journey proves that in the futility of man's spiritual blindness and frailty of his limited, microscopic intellect, faith in God will lead him into the possession of the eternal promises of God.

FAITH AND OBEDIENCE

While it is important that we recognize that Abraham simply did what God said, we should also recognize that one of the igniters of faith is obedience. **"Now the Lord said unto Abram, get thee out of thy country, and from thy kindred, and from thy father's house, unto a land I will show thee."** *Genesis 12:1* We have seen the fire of faith, but have we seen what ignited it? God spoke and gave Abraham a command. It is evident that once you analyze the human mind as it relates to the unknown versus the known, we tend to gravitate toward the known or the familiar.

We shouldn't overlook the humanity of Abraham and treat him as some robotic automaton. He had spiritual, psychological, and emotional ties to his homeland this was an issue, as it would be for most human beings. Abraham grew up in his homeland with his family. It was the only place he had ever called home. Abraham's homeland was his place of birth, development, growth, education, prosperity, inheritance, and religion.

He was told by God to give up everything to go somewhere which his compass registered as nowhere. He was told to forsake all that was familiar, known, tried, inspected, tested, and guaranteed to him. The familiar is where man is comfortable. At home he does not have to acquire new skills, deal with change, or encounter inconvenience. He is the most secure where he perceives his stability and inheritance to be.

ABRAHAM HAD TO LEAVE ALL

Moving for Abraham was a radical upheaval of his normal life. He not only was to embrace a new country, but a new system of worship of the true God. **"And Joshua said unto all the people, thus saith the Lord God of Israel, your fathers dwelt on the other side of the flood in old time, even Terah the father of Abraham, and the father of Nachor and they served other gods."** *Joshua 24:2* Abraham descended from a lineage that worshipped idol gods. His native religion deified false gods. He grew up with and around idols. His relative experience to a supreme being was through the false, phony, counterfeit worship of graven and molten images of gods conjured up by demons and the human imagination. How could he know about Canaan? How could he know about Jehovah the self-existent, eternal God in a land of false gods?

Abraham didn't know anything about Canaan or Jehovah. What prompted him to move? What is the basis of his faith? Abraham moved without the benefit of concrete, physical, natural, and intellectual data. Obedience and faith go hand in hand. What do you do when you don't see the outcome of a situation, but God tells you to do it anyway? Obey God! *Your obedience is a trigger for the full release of faith. Obedience is like pulling the trigger on a gun. When you pull the trigger, the bullet of faith will be fired.*

Abraham didn't understand; but through his obedience, he demonstrated faith while he was intellectually, emotionally, and spiritually blind. **"By faith Abraham, when he was called to go out into a place which he should after receive for an inheritance, obeyed, and he went out, not knowing whither he went."** *Hebrews 11:8* His faith in the unknown was demonstrated by obedience. We must learn how to obey God in the darkest, most dim lit and dreary situations. Our father is looking to receive from us what Abraham demonstrated - *obedience*. Our psycho-spiritual, analytical rationale is foolishness to God. God is no more impressed by your intellect than he is by a three-ring circus of elephants.

God's promises are for those who are obedient and faith-filled. **Obedience says that I have faith and faith says that I will be obedient.** Abraham didn't know more academically, theologically, spiritually, intellectually, or geographically. However, he did know how to obey and how to have faith in the invisible, eternal, omnipotent, majestic Jehovah God. His obedience and faith prompted him to simply do what God told him to. Abraham knew how to obey and have faith in God.

THE REVELATION OF GOD TRANSCENDS TRADITION

Truthfully, you will not move to the next level in God or cross over into the realm of promise until you make a move. We need to move from bad traditions, superstitions, myths, wise tales, ideologies, antique methodologies, old mindsets, and other unproductive thoughts, habits, and ways that are keeping us from inheriting the full benefits of being a part of the Kingdom of God.

It amazes me how people are loyal to theology that has been handed down to them. I call it **"Hand-Me-Down Theology"**. Have you ever been a part of a family that was poor and couldn't buy new clothes? So they saved the original clothes they purchased for the older children and passed it down to the younger ones, whether it fit or not. The older children wore it first then the younger ones would wear all of the older sibling's clothes. If you were a part of a big family and you were one of the younger siblings, usually by the time it got to you, it was old, dingy, stained, too big, too small, and sometimes mangled. But because it was handed down and money was tight, you wore it.

"Hand-Me-Down Theology" in this discussion is an erroneous belief in or about God that was adopted by a prior generation or organization, but is totally unsubstantiated by Scripture and usually filled with the opinions of men as they sought to discern God usually with a lack of understanding. The theology is passed down from generation to generation and is usually added to or guarded by the next generation of organized believers. The present/current generation or organization that upholds the **"Hand-Me-Down Theology"** feels that if they abandon the original, erroneous theology, then they will lose their identification with past pioneers of the organization and would somehow comprise themselves as an organization and even compromise their faith.

One of the most tragic things about **"Hand-Me-Down Theology"** is that the followers usually worship the founders and pioneers of the organization that is more known for their theological beliefs than God. Instead of them referring to God or what His Word says about particular beliefs, they refer to what the founder or even the organization says and this is pitiful. We have made gods out of messengers and put God Himself in a box. In order for some to move forward, they must move away from a **"Hand-Me-Down Theology"** to the correct context and interpretation of the pure Word of God.

BAD TRADITIONS BRING BONDAGE AND ERROR

It sickens me to see God's people live in bondage because of **"Hand-Me-Down Theology"**. This theology that has been adopted as Scripture and law is usually legalistic bondage which affects the quality of life of those who uphold these beliefs. It also impairs the ability of its followers to see God in His purest light and embrace Him. Those who preach and perpetuate **"Hand-Me-Down Theology"**, whether they be sincere or not, usually become oppressors and taskmasters demanding submission to what they preach or offering doom and spiritual demotion in return to those who don't abide by their beliefs.

Many people in the body of Christ are bound and have the most warped, twisted, crooked view of God. Our views of God affect our perception of and reception of promises from God. Many are trying to have faith in a web of **"Hand-Me-Down Theology"** and are falling short in receiving their full inheritance because preachers are not preaching just the Word of God. They have injected the filler material of **"Hand-Me-Down Theology"** and this is preventing God's people from seizing all that God freely gives to them.

Many preachers and believers of **"Hand-Me-Down Theology"** fight what they haven't experienced and will go to the grave defending gross error. I wish I had more time to deal with this subject, but let me share a few Scriptures with you. *Mark 7:9-13* is a passage where Jesus is challenging man's traditions which violate the very Word of God. The Ten Commandments given by Moses instructs children to honor their Father and Mother. The children had an obligation regardless of age, marital status, etc. to honor, respect, help, and assist their parents.

It is apparent that the Pharisees and other groups, who supposedly were guardians of the Law, were violating the commandment of honoring their parents by declaring that what they owned was "corban" - meaning it was dedicated to the temple as a gift and could not be used to take care of their parents. In reality, the Pharisees and others were declaring "corban", but were selling their possessions and using the proceeds for their own selfish purposes omitting to care for their parents; thus violating the commandment of God. In *Mark 7:13* Jesus declares, **"Making the word of God of none effect through your tradition, which ye have delivered and many such like things do ye."** The Amplified Bible states it like this, **"Thus you are nullifying and making void and of no effect [the authority of] the Word of God through your tradition, which you [in turn] hand on. And many things of this kind you are doing."**

Man can insert his opinions that quickly become **"Hand-Me-Down Theology"** which is accepted as doctrine and nullifies the authority of the Word of God. Man takes his opinion of the Word of God, hands it on to others, and eventually it becomes a tradition. This is not in contradiction with *Isaiah 55:11* where God declares, **"So shall my word be that goeth forth out of my mouth, it shall not return unto me void, but it shall accomplish that which I please, and it shall prosper in the thing whereto I sent it."** When God sends His Word it accomplishes what it is purposed to do. But when we add to what He has said and it is in contradiction to the proper context and interpretation, we hinder the Word from being effective within the intent it was applied.

We have lumped opinions, ignorance, cultural ideologies, superstitions, philosophy and other things in with the Word of God. This affects the harvest potential of the Word because people are trying to grasp God's Word, but it has been mixed with opinion and watered down with cultural tradition. As a result, many don't see the harvest or the power of God's Word. We can't add to what He said and expect to get the full benefits. The opinions of man are finite and rely strictly upon the power of the one who created it; but the Word of God is infinite and is empowered by the living God.

GOD'S WORD AND TRADITION DON'T MIX

Many times leaders consciously or unconsciously do like the Pharisees and take a Biblical law or principle and add in personal commentary which is unsubstantiated by Scripture. They make it a law and over time it becomes the doctrinal position of their group, sadly to the detriment of its followers. When the followers try to apply the principles to every day life, the opinions of men added to the Biblical text do not render the return they anticipated, even though the basis of it is grounded in Scripture. You can't fry chicken in water and you can't wash dishes with oil. The Word of God has a specific purpose that it has been created for. If you misuse or mishandle it, you won't see the fruit it has been designed to produce.

God didn't want Abraham to become entangled in the bad traditions and **"Hand-Me-Down Theology"** of his native land; so He called him out. If God tells you, like Abraham, to get out, then you better do it. Don't spend one more second in a place out of which God has called you. Don't waste another day in a place from which God has told you to move. If God said go, then go. Don't hang around for the finale. Tell that situation, "I sympathize with you, but I must go. I love you, but I must go. I appreciate you, but I must go. You got me started, but I must go."

Your first step to enter into your promised land is to move. Tell mama and papa bye and then go because until you move from where you are now, you will never receive the promise. Move from negative thinking. Move from poisonous friends. Move from bad associations. Move from pessimistic people. Move from dead-end jobs. Move from dead religion. Move from dead churches. Move! Move! Move! Pack your bags, saddle your horse, load your car, get those who are meant to go with you, and move!

Abraham accepted the pure word of God and that was enough. He broke ties with his homeland, native religion, and changed addresses to a city whose builder and maker was God. If you knew what Abraham did, you wouldn't question God about not having enough money for the project, building, or business. If you knew what Abraham did, pastors you wouldn't seriously question if the church will grow, prosper, survive, or thrive. If you knew what Abraham did, you wouldn't question the unseen places of ministry, unusual giving, or humanly far-fetched, out-of-sight things He is leading you to do right now. If you knew what Abraham did, you wouldn't constantly question God about your abilities and make excuses for not doing what He has called you to do.

If you want to please God, prosper, pursue purpose, and reach your destiny, you are going to have to know what Abraham knew. ***Abraham knew what God said and he knew by faith that God could be trusted to keep His word.*** If you know what God said and if you know He can be trusted, then you can be a father of a nation that God will raise up out of your loins. If you know what God said and you trust Him, then you will start walking right now and you won't stop until you get to your preordained, predestined land of promise. I'm not saying there won't be obstacles. I'm not saying you won't falter; but if you know what Abraham knew, you'll get up by faith and you won't let anything stop you from moving toward the promise.

PERSONAL REFLECTIONS

Please feel free to discuss these questions with friends, family or a small group. Search yourself with an open heart and let God fill your every need and desire.

1. How do you view Abraham in comparison to yourself?
2. Abraham had to bury his father and move toward his destiny. Have you figuratively or literally ever had to bury something or somebody and move forward?
3. What simple thing did Abraham do that made him a great man of faith?
4. Do you consider yourself to be obedient to God?
5. Abraham had to let go of his home-land and move forward by faith in God. What makes it hard for you to let go when God speaks?
6. What is Hand-Me-Down Theology as defined by the author?
7. How have you been affected by Hand-Me-Down Theology?
8. What traditions have you been taught that don't line up with God's Word?
9. How much of what you believe now is Hand-Me-Down Theology or Scripture?

INTIMATE REFLECTIONS

Abraham was a mere mortal whose relationship with God transcended mortality. We must remember that the people we read about in the Bible were flesh and blood just like us. Abraham distanced himself from others in the human race because he had an incredible ability to have faith in God. His obedience triggered a faith that hasn't been surpassed by any. He simply obeyed and believed God. We search for the needle in the haystack that will completely alter our lives forever when really it is the haystack itself. Most of our problem isn't with misunderstanding it is with what we refuse to do with what we understand. God birthed a covenant relationship with Abraham that would travel through his bloodline to unlimited generations. He didn't become a legend because he avoided hard choices. Abraham had to abandon his home and native religion to become a father of many nations. What ancient, irrelevant, traditional information about God do you need to abandon?

REFLECTIONS JOURNAL

Chapter 5

FAITH IS

Now faith is the substance of things hoped for the evidence of things not seen. Hebrews 11:1

The working definition of faith has been explored for centuries. The value of faith and the study of it have proved to be without measure and, at times, exhaustless. Faith is not just the connecting thread between man and his creator. Faith is also power that connects man to his potentiality and enables him to release it into productive expression. You cannot achieve in life unless you have faith in the abilities God gave you. Those abilities could range from leadership to creativity; but whatever they are, faith will empower you to use them.

FAITH BRINGS YOU INTO THE REALITY OF GOD

You cannot know God without faith. *Hebrews 11:6a* says **"But without faith it is impossible to please him: for he that cometh to God must believe that he is."** The upcoming chapter on faith and patience briefly discusses the incomprehensibility of God by using the senses. Man's link to the father is through his faith. The God of all creation exists on a plane of reality beyond the scope of our sensory mechanisms. The spiritual is not only a plane of intangible, ethereal light, but is actually a universe itself that is inhabited by beings. Spiritual beings occupy the spiritual universe.

The Spiritual universe is composed of what could probably be best described as spiritual matter. It is a cosmos within itself that actually exists with an order of inhabitants and kingdoms, but it exists on another dimensional plane. (Colossians 1:16) Faith transports and connects us from the physical, material universe to the spiritual universe. The faith-figures of the Bible didn't have the 66 books of canon, nor were Old Testament Patriarchs empowered through the Holy Spirit daily.

So what did they have? They had faith in God. When referring to Abraham in the book of *Hebrews 11:8-10,* the Bible records that, **"By faith Abraham, when he was called to go out into the place which he should after receive for an inheritance obeyed and he went out not knowing whither he went. By faith he sojourned in the land of promise, as in a strange country, dwelling in tabernacles with Isaac and Jacob, the heirs with him of the same promise. For he looked for a city which hath foundations whose builder and maker is God."** Abraham left home not knowing where he was going.

How often has God spoken a command to us and we felt like more instructions were necessary? We wanted a sign from God. We even fasted, prayed, and sought Him for more clarity. There is nothing wrong with being sure, but some of our attempts are faithless, fearful reactions to the unknown. Our feeling usually is that if we could just see a little clearer or maybe if we had more information, we would feel more comfortable.

GOD'S COMMAND IS FOOLISHNESS TO MAN

Many times when God speaks to us, we don't know how we are going to get to the predestined place. He usually doesn't give complete instructions concerning the date, time, place, and methodology to be used to connect you to the manifested promise. Many times He will tell you to step out and do something without giving you step-by-step instructions. He will tell you to pursue something that is so big until you can't even imagine yourself with it. What He says many times defies systems of logic and reason. To us His plans are ridiculous, absurd, astronomical, and like with Sarah - comical making us laugh at the very thought of it.

Has God ever told you to do something so far-fetched that you laughed? You know — like starting a church with no members (Ha! Ha! Ha!), or pursue a colossal, church building with a small membership (Ha! Ha! Ha!), or purchase a million dollar facility with a yearly budget of less than $100,000 (Ha! Ha! Ha!), or quit a lucrative job and go full-time in ministry with no contacts (Ha! Ha! Ha!), or even go tell a complete stranger a word from God (Ha! Ha! Ha!)

Sometimes things He tells us to do will cause us to not only laugh, but also stutter and temporarily lose our trend of thought. I have literally been dazed after God spoke and confirmed something within me. My attempts to analyze what He said have been so overwhelming until my mind strained itself in trying to grasp the immensity, possibility, and complexity of the promise He spoke concerning my life.

Abraham had been given a command to take his family and leave a place he knew everything about and go to a place he knew nothing about. He left a place he was conscious of and headed toward a place he was unconscious of. **"He looked for a city which hath foundations, whose builder and maker was God."** He searched for a city, a place of abode in which God created for him. His intellect was useless, a compass was needless, and a map was pointless. His journey would be taken by faith.

THE DEFINITION OF FAITH

So what is faith? The conventional definition of faith is *allegiance to duty or a person, loyalty, belief and trust in God, complete trust.* Let's look at *Hebrews 11:1*. It says, **"Now faith is the substance of things hoped for the evidence of things not seen."** I believe that this verse is a good, working, Biblical definition of faith. The Amplified Bible says it like this, **"Now faith is the assurance (the confirmation, the title deed) of the things [we] hope for, being the proof of things [we] do not see and the conviction of their** reality [faith perceiving as real fact what is not revealed to the senses]."

The conventional definition mentions words like allegiance, belief, and complete trust in defining faith. The Amplified Bible stresses faith as being the assurance, confirmation, even holding the title deed, and having proof of what you hope for with a conviction perceiving facts that haven't been revealed to the senses. Wow! Let's look at the significant words in the verse. **"Now faith is the substance of things hoped for the evidence of things not seen."**

The word "faith" comes from the Greek word *pistis* which means credence or conviction of religious truth of God. When one has faith, the conviction or inner convincing is analogous with a convicting of a criminal in court. The prosecutor must have evidence that convinces a jury or judge that the suspect is guilty. The proof is not in hear-say, conjecture, or circumstantial evidence; but a true case has physical, tangible, certifiable facts that prove guilt.

When one has faith, he is convinced by his belief in God and this gives him evidence to support his belief. The word "substance" comes from the Greek word *hupostasis* which means a setting under (support), concrete, essence, assurance, or confidence. The word "hoped" comes from the Greek word *elpizo* which means to expect or confide or trust. The word "evidence" comes from the Greek word *elegchos* which means proof or conviction.

Paraphrasing *Hebrews 11:1*: Now **faith** — a credence or conviction of religious truth of God is the **substance** — a setting under (support), concrete, essence, assurance, or confidence of things **hoped for** — expected or have confidence in or trusting for and the **evidence** — proof or conviction of things not seen (invisible). *Faith is a conviction concerning God that is set under, under-girded, supported, and assures of things expected and has proof or evidence that is a conviction or convincing that the invisible things we expect and believe God for are unseen, but yet a reality.*

So now that you have a better understanding of how God defines faith, let's briefly see how it is relevant to our daily life. I am not making an attempt to paint God as a genie who is strictly available to grant wishes. I promote getting to know God first through establishing a relationship with Him. As a result of this and His covenant with you, He will add things in your life. (Matthew 6:33) Since our relationship with God is based first on faith, we must arm ourselves properly with the knowledge of how to skillfully use it.

THE RELEASE OF FAITH

I am only attempting to cover one mode of how we release faith to connect with God. When we pray, faith must be utilized to get results. *Mark 11:24* says, **"Therefore I say unto you, what things soever ye desire when ye pray, believe that ye receive them and ye shall have them."** How does faith work in the realm of prayer? For example, let's say that you are seeking God for financial increase in your life.

First, you believe that as a child of God, you are entitled to an increase. You give tithes and offerings to the Lord. You recognize that according to *Malachi 3:10* as a result of honoring Him with tithes and offerings, He promised to open the windows of Heaven and pour you out blessings you will not have room enough to receive. You must also embrace *3 John, verse 2* which declares that God wants you to prosper.

Second, you also recognize numerous other scriptures exist to support your expectations as a child of God to walk in prosperity spirit, soul, and body. I could give you more information, but let's just go to number three. (Deuteronomy 8:18; 28:12-13)

Third, realize that you must recognize how faith works with the Word of God. Your prayer is for financial increase. So here is how faith works. Remember the definition of faith: "Now **faith** — a credence or conviction of religious truth of God is the **substance** — a setting under (support), concrete, essence, assurance, or confidence of things **hoped for** — expected, have confidence in, or trusting for and the **evidence** — proof or conviction of things not seen (invisible)."

God's Word is a guarantee that what you have faith for, you will receive. Let's apply your request for financial increase to *Hebrews 11:1*. "Now **faith** — a conviction of religious truth of God even His Word and power to give you [increase] is the **substance** — is set under (supported), assured, or confident **of things** [the increase]

hoped for — expected or confident in and the **evidence** — proof [possession of my conviction or convincing about God and His power to give increase] of **things** — [the increase] not seen." What I am convinced about cannot be seen with the natural eye, but is real. Your faith in God is supported and assured confidently with proof of your conviction about your belief in God for [increase] — proof that cannot be seen in the natural realm, but is real.

In plainer terms, when you have faith in God for something, the evidence exists inwardly within your heart before it is manifested outwardly. When I refer to the heart, I am speaking of your mind. I believe that man is a three-dimensional being, spirit, soul, and body. (1 Thessalonians 5:23) I also believe that at conversion the Spirit of God comes into your spirit and regenerates it. You are then sanctified or set apart. The mind, which is contained within the soul where intellect, will, and emotions reside, has to be transformed and renewed so you can begin to take on the mind of Christ. (Romans 12:2)

The spirit is where I commune and embrace the mystical. And the renewed mind is where I affirm and confirm my experiences. I believe that the renewed mind embraces the mystical and connects to it by faith through the spirit. The mystical is the spiritual and in this discussion is relative to our interaction with God who is a spirit. (John 4:24)

So if I believe God for increase, once I pray and have faith, the increase is contained in my heart/mind where I am convinced. The increase I have faith for which is contained in my heart is the evidence.

Let me pause to inform you that to God, what is in your heart is just as concrete, substantive, real, and as tangible as physical things are in the natural. *Matthew 5:27-28* **"Ye have heard that it was said by them of old time, thou shalt not commit adultery. But I say unto you, that whosoever looketh on a woman to lust after her hath committed adultery with her already in his <u>heart</u>."** The prophet Samuel had to educate Jesse and his sons as to how God selects kings. *2 Samuel 16:7* says, **"But the Lord said unto Samuel, look not on his countenance or on the height of his stature because I have refused him, for the Lord seeth not as** man seeth, for man looketh on the outward appearance but the Lord looketh on the <u>heart.</u>"

When you believe something whether it is bad or good, it is in your heart. And not only does God know it, but to Him your thoughts are actions. You may say, "I thought it, but I didn't do it." To God, you did it. *The evidence of what we believe for is not contained within the confirmation of external sources. What we believe God for in our heart is the evidence.*

Fourth, you should pray with confidence that your request pleases God and is done according to your faith. 1 John 5:14-15 "And this is the confidence that we have in him, that, if we ask anything according to his will he heareth us. And if we know that he hear us, whatsoever we ask, we know that we have the petitions that we desired of him." I must believe my prayer is valid, legitimate, and answered by God.

Fifth, the increase I have prayed for is real and exists in my heart prior to any visible manifestation. If I continue to have faith in my heart for what I believe, then I have what my faith has selected. As long as I believe, I will receive the manifestation. I have the spiritual evidence, but now I am waiting for the natural manifestation of it. I mentioned in chapter one how things first begin in the invisible and are translated into the visible. *Faith is not guessing or wishing. When you have faith, you have the evidence of what you believe.* Long before the increase is manifested in the natural, it will have already existed as reality in your heart.

So when they ask you did you get the increase and your bank account is not reflective of this, you can say yes because the increase is in the invisible vaults of your heart and will be soon transferred into the visible vaults of your natural bank. External reality is determined by inward reality. The external is determined by what you believe internally. Physical, tangible, manifestations materialize according to the invisible, intangible, inner reality of faith. In simpler terms, what happens outwardly must line-up with what has already happened inwardly.

Faith is a conviction concerning God that is set under, under girded, supported and assures of things expected and has proof, evidence that is a conviction or convincing that the invisible things we expect and believe God for are unseen but yet are a reality.

WHY FAITH? *"Your Guide to Surviving and Thriving in Tough Times"*

PERSONAL REFELCTIONS

Please feel free to discuss these questions with friends, family or a small group. Search yourself with an open heart and let God fill your every need and desire.

1. We cannot know God or connect with Him except by faith. Has God ever said or promised you something that seemed foolish and hard to believe? If so, what?
2. What is the conventional definition of faith?
3. What is the Biblical definition of faith as defined by the author?
4. Outline the steps the author lists that show how faith works in the realm of prayer?
5. Fill in the steps the author lists with one personal request and apply it in your life.
6. How important is it for us to have a conviction about what we believe?
7. Where is the evidence of what we believe?
8. Where do most people look to find the evidence of their faith?
9. How important is it to pray with confidence? Do you have personal challenges praying with confidence? If so, why?

INTIMATE REFLECTIONS

Our understanding of faith in God is crucial if we are going to attain any true measure of success and enjoy it. Faith possesses both evidence and conviction. We must be convinced that God is for us and when we release faith, external things aren't our first-hand source of confirmation. Faith has its' own evidence room which is contained within the heart of man. Once you believe God for something, what happens outwardly will line up with what's in your heart. Believe in the dreams and hopes God has inspired you with and don't back down. Seek God in prayer with confidence knowing in your heart that He hears every word you pray. Face today and tomorrow with a new bold definition of faith and change your world.

REFLECTIONS JOURNAL

Chapter 6

FAITH UNDER FIRE

On June 6, 1944, one of the bloodiest and most intense battles in the history of war transpired. "The Battle of Normandy", also known as D-Day, is a war forever inscribed in the annals of history. The Western Allies in World War II banded together to free Europe from Nazi control. This bloody battle would begin on June 6, 1944 and is said to have ended on June 30, 1944. The invasion was meticulously planned by President Dwight Eisenhower and the military. The Allied Forces prepared a multi-stage, multi-directional strategy that would eventually ensure them victory and push Hitler back into Germany.

 I personally was intrigued by the Allied Forces strategy to invade by sea which meant troops would be airlifted or transported by ships and deployed into water. They would then traverse the various beachheads while simultaneously engaging the enemy in battle. It takes courage to fight in a battle. It takes even more courage to advance up a slippery, sandy beachhead while under attack. I can only imagine what it was like to tread water in the early morning hours and then run up a grainy beach while trying to dodge bullets.

 One statistic suggested that during the first wave of attacks at Juno beach, the Canadians suffered 50% casualties. The open beachhead exposed the Allied Forces to Nazi soldiers who were already positioned behind fortified barriers. It was very difficult for the Allied Forces to navigate through a barrage of bullets and bombs.

Persistence and the overwhelming numbers of Allied troops eventually turned the tide on the beaches of Normandy.

YOUR PERSONAL D-DAY

Have you felt as if your life is a beach in Normandy during World War II and every thing you attempted to do is under attack? Life presents us with situations that feel like a steep, difficult, unforgiving terrain. Trying to climb up the hill of life to gain success is difficult when creditors are after us, disease assaults our bodies, loved ones die, tragedy leaves us penniless, and psychological dysfunctions challenge our will to live. I personally believe that the battle is the Lord's, but that doesn't mean that we don't have our own level of warfare. *1 Timothy 1:18* **"This charge I commit unto thee, son Timothy, according to the prophecies which went before on thee, that thou by them mightest war a good warfare."**

The battle is ultimately between God and the devil, but as children of God we are very much involved in this epic struggle. I want to be very frank in saying that I am not the kind to spiritualize everything, but the Bible clearly states the devil is real and he is our adversary. (John 8:44; 1 Peter 5:8) We must be aware that evil is a real force and put up a good fight.

Sometimes when we teach on faith and what it can accomplish we forget to inform you that your faith will experience some adversity. I personally consider myself to be a hope dealer. I believe that my main assignment is to point people to Christ and give them hope. In all of my faith and optimism I would be remiss if I didn't tell you that sometimes you will do all that you can and it seems as if nothing is working. Living a life that is pleasing to God doesn't exempt you from pain, suffering, and trials. Living a life of faith doesn't mean you will be removed from being pursued by evil. Reading the Bible, fasting, praying, giving, etc. does not absolve you from the attack of the enemy. Feeding the poor and helping the needy doesn't excuse you from being affected by tragic experiences. We must be prepared for the sound and fury of machine guns blazing, grenades exploding, and snipers perched atop a high hill all with one objective to destroy us. We need a faith that is forged in struggle, tested in battle, and equipped to confront any situation.

EXPECT A CHALLENGE

Faith doesn't guarantee us a utopia-like existence that will be free from all the challenges of life. If anything, people of faith will see the bull's-eye get bigger on their chest. We must know that even when something is given by God, there will be an attempt by our adversaries to steal it. *1 Peter 4:12* **"Beloved, think it not strange concerning the fiery trial which is to try you, as though some strange thing happened unto you."** Just like the valiant advancing allied soldiers on the beaches of Normandy, we will be tried. So don't be surprised when opposition comes. Be prepared to stare it down and conquer it.

Job 5:7 says, **"Yet man is born unto trouble, as the sparks fly upward."** The Amplified Bible says, **"But man is born to trouble as the sparks and flames fly upward."** Mankind's encounter with trouble is as certain as fire burning up. Just as we can count on fire ascending with plumes of smoke upward, we can be certain that trouble will exist parallel to the human race. Regardless of your theological, psychological, spiritual, and intellectual background or belief, trouble will find you.

MORE TROUBLE FOR THE PRODUCTIVE

Trouble is an equal opportunity hunter in that it stalks all who exist regardless of gender, ethnicity, religion, or creed. I do believe that people who are productive and striving to make an impact on this world experience more trouble in forms of adversarial opposition. My premise for this statement is that *"something" is a threat, "nothing" isn't*. Typically people who are doing "nothing" create very few enemies because their "nothingness" is generally only affecting them. "Something", on the other hand, is automatically detected on someone's radar and is observed by forces of good and evil. When "something" is impacting people, it can automatically become a threat to spiritual, political, social, and economic agendas.

I want to use a simple example to make my case in point. Please don't be offended by my simple analogy because I mean no harm. I am going to use what society has labeled as a homeless bum. Again, I repeat, I have respect for all people and I am not belittling or degrading any human being. It is sad to say, but homeless people are many times standing right in front of us, but invisible. Society has written off homeless people because they generally don't have a job, income, home, or means of providing for themselves. Their lack of stability and economic prowess demeans and degrades them in the eyes of many people. They are seen as derelicts, rejects, and objects of pity and disdain.

When people pass a homeless person on the street, they usually fear being asked for money or robbed. Typically, homeless people are looked upon as unimportant, non-productive, undesirables in our society. The world passes them by daily except when they sleep where they shouldn't or infringe into areas that are off limits. Otherwise, homeless people are seen, but not seen.

What if a homeless person started cleaning himself up? What if he got a job? What if he got a place to stay? Cleaning himself up makes him a little more visible to the general public. Getting a job puts him in the path of competition in the market place, elevates him into the status of acceptable, and he is on his way into normality. Finding a place to stay removes him from an environment of obscurity into a dwelling place with other socially acceptable, normal people.

He is now visible, normal, and socially accepted. People are less likely to walk past him. They will actually look at him on the street, at work, and in the neighborhood where they live. That same person becomes attractive to many others who now desire his friendship or companionship. That same homeless person is now on the radar in the dating market, job market, housing market, etc. and has officially entered into the competitive rat race as a threat.

There are more people competing with the average citizen for a job, house, or loan than those trying to take a homeless persons make-shift bed or place in line at the soup kitchen. People who are visible and acknowledged as productive are a threat to others. People who have great influence are a threat to other people who have counter distinctive agendas.

I make it my point to avoid endorsing any particular political candidate or party. I am quite aware of the impact politics has on the world and the various microcosms it affects including the church. I ultimately believe that it is my obligation as a minister of the gospel to assist and advise both parties. I don't mind inviting candidates to speak at the church or commenting on unsavory things in the political realm. After presenting the candidates to the congregation or personally commenting on political matters, I then let the people decide for themselves what their vote or opinion will be.

Admittedly, I am highlighting politics to make my next point. The 2008 campaign produced a cadre of interesting characters. The final three front-runners during the rewriting of this book are John McCain for the Republicans, a long time U.S. Senator with a distinguished record; Hillary Clinton, a former president's wife and U.S. Senator; and Barack Obama, a young U.S. Senator from Illinois who is a few years into his federal political career. John McCain and Hillary Clinton have been news headliners for years, but Barack Obama just became noticed by the national media during his campaign for senator and subsequently after the amazing speech he gave at the Democratic National Convention.

Before he became senator, many Illinois residents knew who he was. But since he became a front-runner for president within the Democratic Party, millions now recognize him. This recognition has caused him to be scrutinized by politicians, religious leaders, reporters, talk show hosts, and pretty much anyone who can talk. John McCain and Hillary Clinton have had their share of scrutiny and attacks from various sources. But now because Barack Obama is running for president with success, the whole world is conscious of who he is, including the people who have agendas that are threatened by his. Success brings both supporters and hecklers. Success makes both new friends and new enemies.

Amazingly, people are talking about Barack Obama who never met him. While he was just an Illinois state politician, he wasn't impacting the nation; but as soon as he gained a national following and became a threat to win the National Democratic Nomination for President, it seems as if everyone has an opinion of who he is, what he's done, and what he can do.

TROUBLE FOR THE GIFTED

Is it me or do gifted people seem to have the most difficult time? I typically shudder to use Hollywood as an example of anything truly noteworthy, but one thing that is certainly true is that it contains many talented and gifted individuals. It appears that much of the soiled, tainted news of foul-ups, drug addiction, etc. on American news comes from alleged Hollywood stars and socialites. Of course this type of activity isn't limited to Hollywood. It isn't a coincidence that some of the world's most gifted actors, producers, writers, or directors seem to always grace the covers of news magazines, tabloids, internet sites, and even headline the evening news because of their exploits.

One actor/writer/producer in particular, who I have a great deal of respect for, was arrested for drunk-driving and during the process was spewing forth racial epithets about the Jews. This event occurred after he presented the world, in my opinion, with the greatest and most successful movie about Jesus Christ that has ever been made.

I could give example after example about politicians, athletes, etc. to further cement my point, but I won't. I prefer to refer to the Holy Writ instead. The Bible is replete with people who were gifted and encountered much trouble. One of my favorite Bible characters is David. He was a gifted shepherd, musician, warrior, administrator, and worshipper who loved God, but his life was filled with trouble.

At your leisure read about his life in the books of *1&2 Samuel*. It seems that from the minute David was anointed king in the midst of his brothers in *1 Samuel Chapter 16,* his life would be filled with great challenges afterwards. He had to endure giants and jealousy from King Saul. He had to leave his family, native land, and best friend. He lived in dens and caves as a fugitive for several years. He had to deal with the loss of possessions and family at Ziklag. He had to face his own sins because he committed adultery with Uriah's wife and had him executed. Then he eventually was betrayed by his son Absalom, who tried to take his kingship. And David also experienced a host of other issues too numerous to name in this space.

It is true that David brought some things upon himself with the decisions he made. It is also quite evident that when David was anointed as king by Samuel, he became a threat to Saul's agenda and his life would get more complicated.

Search the annals of history and see how those who have made a legendary impact on this world have endured and overcome great opposition and struggle. Search your own family tree. The truly multi-talented and gifted are tempted, tossed, and challenged in unusual ways.

D-DAY NOW

It is possible that you are reading this book during your excursion up the beaches of Normandy in life. Many people are under assault while trying to provide for family, educate themselves, master their personal insecurities, help others, and lead followers into a place they have never been before. It is true that life can pose circumstances that seem to be unfair. Single mothers are trying to juggle work, recital lessons, football practice, college, and parenting while simultaneously trying to keep themselves happy and fulfilled. Some two-parent families are doing all they can with combined incomes and excessive vocational obligations to keep their families from both financial and emotional bankruptcy.

A couple right now is trying to function in life while at the same time trying to piece together a marriage that is shattered into millions of bits and pieces. It was a marriage that appeared to be destined like a fairy tale; but lately it's a nightmare that has drained the life, joy, peace, and excitement from living. Don't even mention the people-helpers — civic leaders, counselors, pastors, assistants, caretakers, supervisors, foremen, etc. who sacrifice themselves for people that eventually try to destroy them.

Life sometimes appear as if it is filled with steep, grainy beaches where the adversary is perched atop a superior position with a sniper's rifle releasing wave after wave of bullets at us. We are all trying to advance up that beachhead in life to move to a better position and overcome our enemies, but it doesn't come without the price of opposition.

HOPE UNDER SIEGE

The book of ***Proverbs 13:12a*** says, **"Hope deferred maketh the heart sick."** Facing the challenge is sometimes easier said than done. It is no small feat to remain encouraged when our lives seem to be filled with more tragedy and trouble than triumph. Sometimes delayed gratification creates opportunities for despair to complicate our emotional state. It is amazing how numerous failures can cause the pendulum of our emotions to swing from courage to discouragement. Once our courage begins to deplete, then it unleashes a series of poisons against our belief system.

Discouragement usually brings depression which releases a vicious attack on hope and faith. Life's battles wear us down at times causing our hope and faith to become vulnerable. During the writing of this revised book, we are experiencing what appears to be a recession. The economy has lost its vitality and people are being affected around the nation. Economic woes nationally usually lead to financial woes personally. Churches are facing financial issues amidst a sputtering economy that is stretching them beyond their limits. People are afraid to spend money for fear of losing what they have. Hardworking, tax-paying citizens are pinching and squeezing purse strings in an attempt to stretch every penny.

Our country has recently participated in a war that has seen over 3,000 of our own soldiers killed in a battle that is yet raging with malicious, explosive violence unleashed on whoever is available to die — man, woman, or child. Our nation is now polarized and strong debate is being waged as to the legitimacy of the war. It is evident that we are dealing with real, poignant, difficult issues.

Despite our present challenges, we must continue to fight valiantly. Our hope and destiny is bigger than our current struggles. We cannot define our present suffering or challenge to be our permanent end. Hope anticipates and prognosticates bigger and better things concerning our future. Faith confirms what hope has provided. Therefore while your faith is under fire, you must learn how to raise your hope higher.

Never forget the outcome of D-Day. The Allied Forces with great numbers, power, skill, and might eventually stormed up those dangerous beachheads and pounded the enemy into submission. Hitler was driven back into Germany and the tide of the war changed in favor of the Allied Forces. The body of Christ is storming the beachheads of life together with divine help and if we keep moving forward, we will enjoy the fruits of a predetermined victory. The D-Days of our life may be challenging, but never forget ***Romans 8:28*** ensures that even the most tragic circumstance must work for our good. What I am saying is that "good" has been hired by God to work for you. All believers operate with "good" as a fixer, reverser, and reciprocator. My hope in God compels me to know that somehow, someway bad must be utilized to bring me good.

After all the misery, pain, and betrayal Joseph experienced, he could still tell his brothers, **"But as for you, ye thought evil against me; but God meant it unto good."** ***Genesis 50:20*** In other words: what you intended for evil, God made it work for my good. I don't know what heinous, horrific evil or what unfortunate things have happened in your life, but I can tell you this: God reverses any curse that attacks His children. You must believe that God will honor His Word and foil the plans of evil in your life. You are a sure thing to win. Losing isn't in your blood or covenant with God. Battles may be lost, but not the war. Whatever comes upon you that was meant to destroy you just like Joseph, God will use it to bring good into your life.

PERSONAL REFELCTIONS

Please feel free to discuss these questions with friends, family or a small group. Search yourself with an open heart and let God fill your every need and desire.

1. What did Paul encouraged Timothy to do in 1 Timothy 1:18? Why is what Paul said important for you?
2. 1 Peter 4:12 and Job 5:7 means what to you?
3. Can you relate in your personal life to the analogy about the homeless person who rises from nothing but once success comes he/she then has all kinds of enemies? How can you relate to this in your life?
4. What gifted people do you know who have a lot of trouble?
5. What is D-Day like in your life?
6. How is your hope? Is it under attack? Who or what is attacking your hope?
7. Joseph experienced evil at the hands of his brothers. What did he say in Genesis 50:20 that helped put his suffering in perspective? Do you believe that what Joseph said applies to your life? How?

INTIMATE REFLECTIONS

If we live long enough, life feels like a war that is out of control. People are facing hardships in life in record proportions. Foreclosures are at an all time high. The climactic pattern has changed so drastically until storms, tornadoes, and hurricanes are pounding man-made structures to a pulp and racking up human casualties in the process. Our financial system is in jeopardy with hard-working people experiencing the worst of a bad economy. Wars loom and are fought daily and morality is under attack. We are definitely living in challenging times. Life at times seems too hard and unfair. We must guard our hope for it is more precious than the gold of Fort Knox. Don't compromise your hope, for when you do, you forfeit your visions and dreams. Remember God is a converter. When life presents evil, He turns it into something good.

REFLECTIONS JOURNAL

Chapter 7

FAITH AND PATIENCE

. ...who through faith and patience inherit the promises.
Hebrews 6:12b

Faith is not glamorous and is not for the faint of heart. To be pregnant with a seed of vision from God but lack resources to see the fulfillment of it, brings challenges. It takes more than a "hallelujah" and a "glory to God" to see your faith bring results. The reality is that many times we have the vision and must wait on the provision. It is a struggle at times to have a vision to build something great for God when your current financial status seems to become more oppressing and depressing by the day. God spoke a word of ministry into your life, but the circumstances of your life just don't add up to produce it.

We may as well be realistic and admit there are times in our lives that frustration enters when the results of our vision haven't arrived. It is difficult to forge ahead when you have believed God for provision, but your current sustenance is barely enough to maintain and is even deteriorating.

When you are pregnant with a vision, God constantly confirms it through the mouths of many witnesses; but sometimes the more they say it is coming to pass, the worse it seems to get. There is nothing more heart-wrenching than when you have been waiting on the Word of God to manifest in your life amidst a reality of lack that can scarcely hold a flicker of hope against hopelessness, but nothing significant happens.

The Rhema Word from the person who prophesied to you is prosperity - spirit, soul and body. But every dimension of your existence indicates that the natural course of events is less than a prosperous present reality. It seems as if while you expect the supernatural, you either get the natural or faint impressions from the supernatural. While you have been exercising faith in God for the overflow, the trickle comes.

I have experienced droughts in my life that were filled with lack-luster, microscopic morsels of hope that could barely feed my personal vision and that didn't begin to scratch the surface in meeting the needs of a God-inspired, international one. Many messages of prophecy have gone forth. They said, "God is going to do it." But after waiting, praying, crying, fighting, and holding on, the question really is, "When?" I have fasted, spoke the Word, attended conferences, abided in my calling, and nothing happened. The inside of my wallet looked the same. The balance on the bank account statement continued to sputter. The bills kept rolling in faithfully and nothing significantly changed.

YOUR SENSES ARE THE ENEMIES OF FAITH

Human senses are more impressed by what they can see. Empirical evidence is what the mind processes. Visible, tangible substance is what the human mind looks to analyze and verify. Many times our delays are visible, living representations to the flesh of our situations. The senses certify what they can see, touch, taste, smell, and hear. If information is beyond the scope of these senses, the flesh cannot affirm it.

It is not surprising how the enemy will attack us. Our senses are powerful guides that enable us to interact, interface, connect, and operate in the physical universe. The information we receive from the senses is real, emotive, and compelling reality. It is hard to deny what you see through your eyes, touch with your hands, taste with your taste buds, smell with your nose, and hear with your ears. If we have the full use of these senses, they are employed every day.

Every morning if you can see, your eyes open bringing the ceiling into view. Your ears bring sounds of the alarm clock, the TV, etc. into hearing. Your nose samples odors in the atmosphere to be processed by the brain - odors like sausage cooking or coffee brewing. Your hands, feet, and arms contain millions of sensory receptors that will interpret touch allowing you to realize that your feet are on the floor and your hands are on the side of bed. Your taste buds enable you to discriminate the minty taste of the toothpaste from the insipid taste of the water swirling around in your mouth.

What God gave us to function with in the physical universe will work against us in the spiritual universe. The physical and spiritual abide on different planes of existence, therefore they are meant to function each in its respective abode. The devil will use the natural to thwart faith and enlist doubt to corrupt it. Since we rely heavily upon our senses to connect with the world around us, they will be utilized every living second.

Although the senses powerfully affect us, the most lethal weapon is the very mind that processes, interprets, and defines information from them. The mind is not only responsible for intellect, but also for emotions. The mind is the intellectual construct which provides us with perspective, consciousness, and the ability to conceptualize enabling us to define reality. Our reality is relative to personal existential experiences. Emotions are a part of this existential journey and provide the fire of stimulus to act, react, believe, or doubt according to the interpretation of empirical data sent to the mind by the senses and processed by it.

In other words, we see it, process it with thought, and carry out our actions with an emotional stimulus as the driving force that adds meaning to it. It is a part of our physical make-up to rely upon the senses and when there is no information for them, they interpret reality accordingly.

The dilemma is that God is undetectable by physical senses and mental faculties. He must be embraced by both the renewed spirit and renewed mind of man. Suffice it to say that He cannot always be detected by the renewed spirit and mind of man. This again justifies the need for faith. The manifestations of our faith are not instantaneously translated into our reality.

We don't usually get the car as soon as we pray for it. It can happen, but many times we wait and then we experience the results of our faith. It is during the waiting period while we are exercising our faith through prayer, declaration, or other divine communicable means that the greatest test occurs. The senses intake information, the mind analyzes it, and emotions give us the stimulus to act, react, or do nothing. So we must contend with the whole process that helps determine our reality.

PATIENCE IS THE ALLY OF FAITH

Patience is a weapon that must be utilized if our faith is going to have longevity and manifest fruit. Let's analyze *James 1:3-4*. It says, **"Knowing this that the trying of your faith worketh patience. But let patience have her perfect work that ye may be perfect and entire wanting nothing."** The conventional definition of patience is *bearing pain or trials without complaint, showing self-control, calm, steadfast, persevering*. The word "faith" comes from the Greek word *pistis* which means credence, conviction of religious truth of God.

The word "patience" as it is used in *James 1:3-4* comes from the Greek word *hupomone* which means cheerful or hopeful endurance, constancy, enduring. The word "worketh" is also used. It comes from the Greek word *katergazomai* which means to finish, fashion, cause, do deed, perform. Paraphrasing *James 1:3,* *"The trying of our assurance, our conviction about God shapes, causes and even employs a cheerful hope that endures with steadfastness, perseverance and self-control."*

If we accept the Word of God and allow it to work, the fruits of its' irrevocable truths will be manifested in our lives. The seemingly abstract, distant, intangible, aloof benefits that the Word of God brings will be realized when it is put into motion by faith. In modern times if someone needed to get from one place to another in a quicker time frame and they utilized the horse and buggy as their primary mode of transportation, it is evident a change would be needed. One might select a car as a potential option in upgrading their mode of transportation. Let's say they choose a car. They go to the car dealer, select a vehicle, and sign the papers. It would appear that the deal is completed, but actually the final phase of the transaction requires that the vehicle be driven off the lot. It is now your property.

This means everything good and bad about the vehicle belongs to you. If it has a super-sized engine with enormous amounts of power or a 25-gallon fuel tank, it would be yours because you signed the papers.

What if after you purchased the car you decided that you didn't want the car? Does that make the abilities and capabilities of the car disappear? No. All the properties of the car would remain in tact. What good would a new or used car be to you if it sat in the driveway and was never driven? To somebody else who would drive the car it would be of great benefit, but to the one who refuses to drive the car it is worthless. In order for you to have your need met of being able to get from one point to another in a shorter amount of time, the purchaser of the car would have to utilize the car by either driving it themselves or employing someone else to drive it. If you want to experience the benefits of God's Word personally, you will have to take the Bible out of the showcase, off the shelf, and use it.

We must make a conscious effort to have faith and believe the results are as the Bible declares. The patience we have should reflect a cheerful, hopeful endurance that has constancy, steadfastness, self-control, and perseverance. Many times we equate patience with just waiting; but many are unfaithful, negative, whining complainers who expect to still receive something from God. Our waiting or demonstration of endurance should be filled with cheer, hope, endurance, steadfastness, constancy, self-control, and perseverance. The devil and people will try our faith and patience, but we must stand upon our conviction with hope that is steadfast knowing that God will respond.

PATIENCE BRINGS US INTO COMPLETENESS

Whatever we believe God for must be accompanied by patience. ***James 1:4*** says, **"But let patience have her perfect work, that ye may be perfect and entire wanting nothing."** The new words introduced into the verse are "perfect" and "entire". The word "perfect" comes from the Greek word *teleios* which means completeness of full age. The word "entire" comes from the Greek word *holokleros* which means complete in every part, perfectly sound or whole. So let's paraphrase the verse. "But let **patience** (a cheerful or hopeful endurance, constancy) have her **perfect** (complete, of full age) **work** (performance) that ye may be **perfect** (complete, of full age) and **entire** (complete in every part, perfectly sound whole wanting (lacking) nothing (none)." In other words, *"Patience brings completeness to the finish work of Christ in our lives and this brings us to completeness, maturity, and soundness with wholeness, wanting for nothing."*

Patience helps exact discipline and mastery over the senses. You learn how to conquer the impulses of the flesh and mental assaults of the enemy and trust God. The process of waiting enables the seed of the Word of God to germinate and replace the thoughts of carnality within the mind. Spiritual growth occurs through a process that is usually initiated by or through our expression of faith.

If you are in it to win it, quitting is not an option when your faith is tested. So you learn how to cheerfully seek God while waiting on the prize. A winner's attitude forces you to be steadfast, creative, resourceful, and humble in seeing the manifestation of your faith. You learn how to see the bright side when there are dark clouds. You learn how to look up when every thing seems to be down. You become a master of optimism when the air is looming with pessimism. Why? Because faith ushers in patience and cheer, but patience is clothing you with a maturity which will wield completeness, soundness, and a wholeness of being that will cause you to lack and want for nothing.

The perfect work of patience is to be done in you. God desires to see us reach maturity in Him. *Ephesians 4:13* says, **"Till we all come in the unity of the faith, and of the knowledge of the Son of God, unto a perfect man, unto the measure of the stature of the fullness of Christ."** If we are to come into maturity or completeness lacking nothing, faith and patience are going to have to be utilized. Not only is our completeness in Him through faith and patience, but also our ability to receive our inheritance of God's promises.

Hebrews 6:12 says, **"That you be not slothful, but followers of them who through faith and patience inherit the promises."** The word "patience" used in this verse is a different Greek word *makrothumia* which means forbearance or fortitude. The definition of "forbearance" is *to refrain from, abstain, to be patient*. The definition of "fortitude" is *strength of mind that enables a person to meet danger or bear pain or adversity with courage*. These definitions are complementary components of patience.

We see the fullness of the concept of patience through the two Greek words employed in this chapter. In ***James 1:3-4*** the Greek word for patience ***hupomone*** denotes cheerful or hopeful endurance, constancy, enduring, an attitude with cheer, expectancy, endurance and constancy. In ***Hebrews 6:12*** the Greek word for patience *makrothumia* denotes forbearance or fortitude. ***True patience is cheerful, hopeful, endurance, and constancy with forbearance, refraining from doing and fortitude or strength of mind enabling a person to bear pain or adversity with courage.*** Let's paraphrase ***Hebrews 6:12***. "That ye be not slothful (lazy) but followers of them who through **faith** (credence, conviction of religious truth of God) and **patience** (forbearance, refrain, abstinence) and fortitude (strength of mind which enables a person to meet danger or bear pain or adversity with courage) and inherit the promises." ***It takes a strong conviction of belief with forbearance and fortitude to obtain the inheritance that God has promised us.***

If you are not determined and willing to believe God and endure the season of waiting, you will not be complete and failure is inevitable. During the course of writing this book, I have had to put the Word of God and many of the principles I have shared with you in this book into practice.

PATIENCE WILL SET YOU UP FOR THE PROMISE

The Lord impressed it upon my heart to start a church in 1998. The task of starting a church from nothing with barely any money was challenging and faith-building. The car my wife and I owned was so ragged it couldn't even take us to church. We started with six adults and a few children in the basement of a home. Over the years we experienced many challenges, but God favored us and we grew. By 2003, the ministry had grown to the point where the church building we were using had outgrown its' usefulness. The Lord spoke to me and said it was time to move. Prior to this, a lovely building went up for sale in our city. This building had everything we needed as a young, growing ministry. But there was one issue, we were small and the price tag was big.

I can vividly remember the pastor of the church that was for sale came and spoke for us. He sat across the desk from me and said, "Anthony I'll make you a good deal on the church." I responded while laughing, "You will, hmm?" At that moment, it was inconceivable and irrational for me to even consider that building. My approach to ministry had been one of faith, but I tried to balance it out with pragmatism. The asking price was $1.2 million. And trust me — if this building were in a large metropolitan area, it would be worth $2.2 million easily. I could not fathom trying to undertake a task with a small, growing congregation that at the time was doing well, but wasn't profiting financially.

Needless to say, I changed the conversation and time moved forward. It was several days afterwards that the Lord challenged and pricked my heart about laughing at the pastor's offer. He immediately begin to speak ***Mark 10:27,*** **"And Jesus looking upon them saith, with men it is impossible, but not with God for with God all things are possible."** He ministered to me several days concerning this verse of scripture and others, but mainly ***Mark 10:27***. I realized that God was challenging me to believe that He could do anything. He instructed me to speak ***Mark 10:27*** three times every time I passed the beautiful church building. It didn't matter how many times a day I passed the building. I was to speak, **"With men it is impossible, but not with God; for with God all things are possible."** I can recall passing by the building after God spoke to me. I began to speak the Word of God and my wife looked at me wondering what I was doing. She eventually began to look forward to me speaking over it.

As the days went by, God settled the issue more and more in my spirit. Eventually I took my former assistant pastor over to the church and we prayed and by faith seized the building. Several weeks later, God put it on my heart to draft a letter to the pastor. I made a proposal and asked him to keep us in mind. It would be several months afterwards before I heard from him.

Many months passed by and many churches toured and looked at the building. Some were serious and a contract was even taken out on the building. In the interest of expediting time, I will skip ahead. During the time when there was a contract on the building, the Lord had placed it within my spirit that it was time to move. Shortly before being prompted to move, the owners of the building we were in began trying to sell it. The situation had moved into the critical stage. We needed another place of worship and we had few options. Our prayer intercessors and the whole church fasted and petitioned God to manifest our faith for this building.

It was during the waning hours of waiting that we discovered another building and were actively pursuing it when something happened that stirred my spirit and caused me to pause. I was troubled about how the process was going with the other building we had in mind and began to tell God I didn't want to miss Him by pursuing this building. Yet we needed a miracle just to get into the one we wanted. We didn't have a million dollars or a down payment to secure a loan. Our church was only five years old at the time. I recall driving around town after a meeting at church to clear my head when I felt compelled to pull up on the lot of the church I really wanted and had been speaking over some 12 to 13 months earlier. I sat on the parking lot in my car and begin to talk to God and ask Him why we couldn't have this building now? He never spoke a word and I drove home.

A few days after driving off the parking lot of the church we wanted, I was at home praying and seeking God concerning the pending business deal for the church and the Lord spoke to me and said to get consultation from two pastors concerning this issue. He instructed me to whom I was to talk to and so I followed up on the Word of the Lord. The first pastor was a friend I have known for some time. He advised me exceptionally in both business and spiritual matters. It was some of the best advice I have ever received from any pastor. I then proceeded to the second pastor who I considered to be a friend and advisor. By the way, the church that he pastored owned the building that I wanted. (Remember, I laughed at him over

12 months earlier.) I didn't call to discuss his building. I called to discuss another business transaction and get his opinion on it.

He gave me some good advice, as I knew that he would and I felt like I could make a better decision after talking to him. As he made his closing statement on what I asked him, he made an opening statement concerning the building they had for sale. One thing that I neglected to mention was that two weeks prior to this conversation, he and I were talking on the phone and he offered me a deal that I felt wouldn't work for us. He immediately reminded me of his offer in our second conversation and sweetened the pot until I couldn't refuse. God soon begin to reveal to me that this was His way of ushering us into a new era with a new building. We went from worshipping in a 2,500-square-feet church to a 28,000-square-feet-church. We now own the facility! We have had our share of challenges, but God continues to intervene and prove that He is with us. The building I spoke to years ago is ours. Guess what I am now speaking — **"PAID FOR!!"**

I believe with all my heart that it is not the will of God for us to pay on it for 30 years. I believe that God is going to open a door for us to own it debt-free, meaning no mortgage and it will be paid for. Faith gave us the title deed and patience ensured that we would wait and not be denied the tangible manifestation of what we believed. Without faith and patience, we would have settled for less than the best.

I don't have all the answers concerning the financial feasibility of purchasing the building, nor do I know exactly how we will receive all the money we need. But I do have one answer — **FAITH IN GOD!** *Mark 10:27,* **"And Jesus looking upon them saith, with men it is impossible, but not with God for with God all things are possible."** *Philippians 1:6* says, **"Being confident of this very thing, that he which hath begun a good work in you will perform it until the day of Jesus Christ."** I have enough FAITH to know God started the process and He will finish it!

I can honestly say that waiting on God by faith with patience brings completeness to the finished work of Christ in our lives. This brings us to completeness, maturity, and soundness with wholeness wanting for nothing. *If you have patience with your faith, you can endure all things, resist the ungodly things, wait on good things, and receive all the things that God has for you.*

WHY FAITH? *"Your Guide to Surviving and Thriving in Tough Times"*

PERSONAL REFELCTIONS

Please feel free to discuss these questions with friends, family or a small group. Search yourself with an open heart and let God fill your every need and desire.

1. Describe how the human senses that God gave us can work against us when we are trying to walk in the Spirit?
2. Have your senses ever deceived you into thinking that the wrong thing was actually right?
3. Have you ever been discouraged by what you could see? If so, how?
4. How does the conventional definition of patience work with what the Bible says in James 1:3-4?
5. The word "patience" in James 1:4 comes from the Greek word **hupomone** which means cheerful, or hopeful endurance and constancy. We should wait with a cheerful attitude. Are you always cheerful while you wait? If not, why?
6. In Hebrews 6:12 another Greek word **makrothumia** is used for "patience". What does it mean? How does this definition affect our ability to be patient?
7. What have you been patiently waiting for?
8. How can patience set you up for the promise?
9. What are you doing to help improve your patience?

INTIMATE REFLECTIONS

The basic ingredients of patience are endurance, waiting, cheer, and fortitude. While many people have endurance, fortitude, and waiting mastered they have neglected cheer. Are you waiting with a negative attitude or with gratitude? We must be careful not to invest precious time in the waiting period only to have our destiny soured by doubt, negativity, and an attitude that reeks of ingratitude. God is constantly looking at our hearts and we must demonstrate with a good attitude that He is worth waiting for. Check yourself now. And if you find a dead cat of ingratitude on the line, remove it and start fresh with a new, better attitude.

WHY FAITH? "Your Guide to Surviving and Thriving in Tough Times"

REFLECTIONS JOURNAL

Chapter 8

FAITH & HOPE

Which hope we have as an anchor of the soul, both sure and stedfast, and which entereth into that within the veil;
Hebrews 6:19

A few years ago, I had the pleasure to travel outside the U.S. with a friend and share the gospel of Jesus Christ. I was given the opportunity to teach and preach in a Pastor's Conference. Pastors came from various cities in this poverty-stricken country to hear the Word of God. They eagerly desired to participate in the conference and be empowered for ministry.

As I was seeking God about what I should share with the people, the subject of faith and hope exploded within my spirit. I was lead by the Spirit of God to inspire hope and faith. It turned out the friend in whom I had traveled with to this conference connected with what God had given me and taught on dreams and not giving up on them. Because our messages were joined - literally married, the Word penetrated the sensitive, hungry, God-loving hearts of the precious pastors who were in attendance. The response to the messages was encouraging.

We were greeted by waves of people who said that they had lost their faith and stopped dreaming. These men and women wore the battle scars of life and bore in their psyche the rigors of political oppression. They had begun to see their faith and hope wilt like grass tossed into an oven. I was honored to witness hope once again fill their hearts and be reflected in the eyes of these wonderful men and women of God. Their wilting hope had begun to resurrect and bloom like wild flowers draped along a beautiful hillside.

Hope, according to **Hebrews 6:19**, is an anchor of the soul. Hope provides stability and vitality for the human race. It is the essential ingredient to living an enjoyable, qualitative life. The modern definition of the word hope is "to desire with expectation of fulfillment or trust, reliance." When a person has hope, they have positive expectations in life and they put trust and reliance in what they are hoping for to become a reality. Imagine what life is like without hope. Most people who commit suicide have lost hope. Life becomes a fleeting option that offers them no reason to hope; so they take their own lives.

Hope and faith are allies in helping us to maintain our connection with God and sustaining the drive for living. It is a fact that the deterioration of the human condition has impacted society in many negative ways. High divorce rates have shredded the family which is the backbone of society, thus creating a myriad of complications. Children now grow up in one parent homes where some become victims of neglect or abuse by the remaining parent or stepparent. Young children are placed in situations where they must deal with adult issues at premature ages. Young boys and girls grow up without the love of both parents and subsequently begin to seek validation and self worth in all the wrong places.

Some have resorted to drugs, alcohol, sex, suicide, same sex relationships, gangs, and other unhealthy ways to self medicate. This experimentation and self-medication with the aforementioned vices isn't limited to young people, but can be witnessed among numerous adults. For many life has been such a tragic disappointment until drastic measures were taken to find answers to relieve the pain.

WARPED PERCEPTIONS

Counseling people for many years has enabled me to have a first-hand look at various angles and experiences of the best and worst of the human condition. It ranges from one or more events to a series of painful events that alters the spiritual and psychological construct of people in negative ways. Once people are damaged spiritually and emotionally, it immediately changes and warps their perceptions of life which in turn negatively impacts their thinking.

When people's perceptions are warped, they began to view life through negative, pessimistic lenses. Every event, good or bad, in life is now passed through a psychological filter that is inherently subjective toward negativity.

Have you ever interacted with people who complained about everything? If things are going well, there is always a "but". What a beautiful day it is, "but". God blessed me with a new job, "but". I really enjoyed the meeting today, "but". Skepticism, ridicule, and pessimism become the companions of the broken and unfulfilled. We must take self-inventory and make sure that our attitude isn't spoiled like last week's ground beef that is sitting in a neglected trash heap. Warped perceptions can lead to spoiled, foul attitudes that drive optimistic people up the wall.

Surrounded by negativity like Saturn's rings, people with negative, warped perceptions live with a theological, psychological, and philosophical bent toward disdain, disgruntlement, and infidelity. I have dealt with gifted, talented, intelligent, hard-working individuals who were capable of doing an excellent job. Despite all the positive qualities, their attitudes were tainted with negativity and therefore inhibited them from being effective in working with people. Their attitudes were so critical, putrid, and anal at times until people shunned working with them. The sobering reality is that if people consistently have problems working with you, the single constant in those situations is you.

Most negative people are self-absorbed and deflect problems back on to people rather than seriously considering themselves as the culprit. The ones who are willing to accept their faults usually swing back and forth like a pendulum between depression and happiness. They are happy until they realize that once again they are the object of criticism and ridicule. Their remorse can cause them to take a downward spiral into depression and be consumed by a barrage of conflicted, negative emotions.

DEPRESSION

- Depressive disorders affect approximately 18.8 million American adults or about 9.5% of the U.S. population age 18 and older in a given year (National Institute of Mental Health).
- Pre-schoolers are the fastest-growing market for antidepressants. At least 4% of preschoolers - over a million - are clinically depressed (Murray and Fortinberry).
- 30% of women are depressed. Men's figures were previously thought to be half that of women, but new estimates are higher (National Institute of Mental Health).
- 80% of depressed people are not currently having any treatment (Agency for Healthcare Research and Quality).
- 92% of depressed African-American males do not seek treatment (Murray and Fortinberry).
- Depression will be the second largest killer after heart disease by 2020. And studies show depression is a contributory factor to fatal coronary disease (Murray and Fortinberry).

The Baker Encyclopedia of Psychology and Counseling says, "Major Depression also called unipolar depression is identified by sad, empty, or hopeless feelings: slowed physical and cognitive behavior, including cognitive disorientation; changes in weight, appetite, and sleeping patterns; diminished interest or pleasure in activities and time spent with friends; and occasional to frequent thoughts of death and suicide." (Lastoria).

Depression affects millions yearly including Christians. I personally believe depression is one of the biggest enemies of mankind. When depression sets in, it gnaws away at the strands of faith in a person's life. Depressed people generally begin to question God, themselves, others, their worthiness, etc. to the point that they begin to wonder about the importance of their existence. When people begin to question the relevance and worth of their existence, usually suicidal thoughts are close by.

Unlike some preachers, I advocate medication when people are accurately diagnosed with a chemical imbalance for depression.

Some people need prescription drugs to help regulate hormones and other pertinent biological chemicals. I believe in miracles, but I also believe that until it manifests, take your prescriptions. It is simply absurd to reject help and yet be sick, ill, or whatever the case is because you are waiting on God. Please don't be insulted. I have prayed for many people and watched God heal them time and time again. I believe in the supernatural power of God. I believe in the power of prayer. It is real! The flip side of the coin is this: I have seen people who were waiting on healing die.

We must approach our issues with a balance and realize a pill or surgery won't stop God if He wants to manifest healing. I am a proponent of faith over man's ability, but we need to utilize wisdom until our faith is strong enough to walk in divine healing.

THE PARASITE OF DEPRESSION

Modern science utilizes a parasite called leeches to help people with various types of blood disorders. Leeches are essentially worm-like creatures that suck blood from their host whether man or beast. Leeches are takers and not givers. They drain the host's blood and if they exist in ample numbers, could slowly kill the host. One of the signs of blood loss is a change of color along with a reduction in energy. People who have lost a lot of blood tend to feel sluggish and eventually have problems walking and performing regular activities.

Depression, like leeches, is a vampirish taker that feeds on the life force of people. It has the power to totally transform vivacious, lively people into fearful, morbid, gloomy zombies. When people are affected by depression, it alters the balance between happiness and sadness and tips the scales toward sadness.

I, like many people, struggled with depression over the years. In recent years, I have embraced my position in the Kingdom of God as an ambassador of Christ. As a result, depression isn't a major factor in my life. When those negative emotions are stirred, I simply refuse to let them dominate my life.

In the earlier years of my walk with God I struggled severely with depression mainly because it crossed over into adulthood from childhood. As a boy and teenager I struggled like most with common depression and occasionally with severe episodes. I remember one such time struggling in my marriage financially, vocationally, and emotionally. I stopped going to church for several weeks. I rarely left the house. At times I couldn't rest and I felt empty inside. Here I was a preacher, father, husband, and child of God struggling everyday to lift my head above water.

At the time, I couldn't figure out what was wrong with me. I had lost my pep, drive, fire, and zest for life. I preferred staying at home in dark rooms with the curtains closed over sunny, summer days outside. Praying was challenging and even heart wrenching. What could I say? What would I pray? Did I really believe anymore? Was I expecting God or failure? When was my marriage going to get better? When were my finances going to get better? When was God going to finally open doors for me to travel, minister, and finally increase my finances? What kind of man was I? Does God really love me? Does my wife really love me? What is my real purpose? Will I always struggle in life? I had so many questions with no answers at an uncertain and tumultuous time in my life.

Finally after several days and multiple weeks went by, my first hero, the first superman I ever knew, namely my father came by to check up on me. I remember sitting in the living room of our tiny apartment when he came in. He asked me how I was doing. I responded passively. We then began to talk. My father is a very educated man who has pastored and counseled people for many years. As I began to describe some of my feelings to him he listened. Finally after listening to my symptoms and feelings, he said, "It sounds like you are depressed." It wasn't that I was so startled at the diagnosis, but it somehow rang a bell. We talked about a few more things and then he advised me on some things that would help me recover.

My father's willingness to help and his easy words of comfort enabled me to accept that I was depressed without making me feel weak or alienated. I took his advice and gradually recovered. I have been blessed to battle many serious battles since that day, but God has brought me to a place in faith that I don't fear or worry. I simply trust God.

HOPE IS THE ANCHOR

It never ceases to amaze me when I have the opportunity to observe ships docked in the harbor how a steel, clunky anchor can help stabilize a ship that weighs several thousand pounds. Despite the instability of the waves, the anchor provides stability to the ship keeping it from drifting. Amazing!

The Bible states in *Hebrews 6:19a,* **"Which hope we have as an anchor of the soul, both sure and stedfast."** As we discussed in an earlier chapter, "hope" comes from the Greek word *elpis* which means the expectation of something good. The word "soul" comes from the Greek word *psuche* which actually describes the mind, will, and emotional realm of man. It is the place where thinking and decision making occurs.

The Amplified Bible states it like this, **"[Now] we have this [hope] as a sure and steadfast anchor of the soul [it cannot slip and it cannot break down under whoever steps out upon it – a hope].."**

I believe that hope helps to anchor, stabilize, and provide steadfastness to the mind of man. Hope keeps the mind always looking for something better. It provides optimism and great expectation amidst life's greatest challenges. Hope is always dreaming and envisioning greater. Hope will always provide reasons to trust God and anticipate light even in the darkest night. Hope ensures that the scale is always positioned where sadness will not outweigh gladness. Hope ensures that the drab and dreary cloak of darkness always contends with at least a pinhead of light.

HOPE IS INVISIBLE

While it is true hope is the anchor of the soul. It tends to elude the skeptic, unbeliever, and rationalist. There are various reasons, some rational and irrational, as to why people struggle with hope. Aside from those who are committed to the power of the human intellect and subsequently define reality by visible, tangible matter, some who have lived with many years of disappointment and emotional oppression usually develop a cynic's mentality about hope.

The Bible discusses the invisibility of hope in *Romans 8:24-25,* **"For we are saved by hope: but hope that is seen is not hope: for what a man seeth, why doth he yet hope for? But if we hope for that we see not, then do we with patience wait for it."**

The pretext of *Romans 8:24-25* exists in verse 23 where Paul is discussing the resurrection of our bodies during the catching away or as we generally say "rapture". He smoothly transitions into a brief exposition of hope itself. We are saved by hope or in this hope. The hope of the redemption or resurrection of the body actually completes the last tense of salvation officially securing the believer for eternity. Believers who died in the Lord will be granted new glorified bodies fit for eternity and totally free from sin.

He delves deeper into hope in verse 24 by saying, **"but hope that is seen is not hope: for what a man seeth, why doth he yet hope for?"** Remember the definition of "hope" which is *the expectation of something good.* The hope or expectation of something isn't rooted in physical reality. It is contained within the realm of thought which is invisible. While it is true that we hope for things that are constructed of physical, tangible matter, it should also be noted that until it materializes and actualizes, we are yet dealing with invisible expectations.

If you were catching a train to a destination, it would have a designated time to arrive. You would adjust your schedule to position yourself to be at the train station before it departs for your destination. While you are waiting at the station whether sitting, pacing, or standing, you would be expecting the train to depart to your destination at a designated time. In other words, you are hoping or expecting to catch a train to your destination. The train is a material object, but your expectation exists within the invisible realm of thoughts. Your expectation of departure on a specific train isn't present in the natural or physical realm while you are waiting for it, but it exists in the invisible realm of thoughts.

Once you board the train and depart, it is no longer hope. Now that the train is here, you are not expecting it because the train is present. What you hoped for that was once invisible, when it arrives actualizes into a verifiable, current reality. The train that you actually hoped for is now present and is no longer a thought of hope, but is now present and accounted for.

We have got to realize that our greatest hopes, dreams, and visions for life shouldn't be forfeited because we haven't seen them manifest. Hope will eventually transport our expectations to the dimensional line that separates the visible from the invisible. Until the appointed time comes, what you hope for must remain in the realm of the invisible.

ATTITUDE OF GRATITUDE

I'm sure many could relate to the train scenario. At some point in life we have had to wait on someone or somebody to transport us to somewhere. I personally don't like to wait long periods of time for people to take me anywhere. For me, time is such a precious asset and an irreplaceable commodity until any minute I have to wait reminds me of how much I could be doing with those fleeting moments.

I must admit in having gained some experience with flight delays and transportation woes, it isn't so much that I have to wait that really complicates my life. It is my attitude while I am waiting that hijacks my peace.

Paul resumes in *Romans 8:25* by saying, **"But if we hope for that we see not, then do we with patience wait for it."** If we have expectations from the invisible and specifically the invisible God, then we must have patience. As we briefly look at the word patience here it comes from the Greek word *hupomone* which means cheerful (or hopeful) endurance, constancy. Paul describes exercising hope with a cheerful, enduring constancy while waiting.

Isn't it amazing that when you constantly stare at your watch marking time, how five minutes can seem like fifteen minutes and an hour may as well be two hours? When we have poor, panic-stricken, ungrateful, impatient attitudes, it is hard to wait for hope to manifest. Generally when we occupy ourselves doing something positive and stop fixating on situations, time seems to advance normally. Impatience is an issue in the world today and especially in the church. If we can't have it now, frustration sets in and people become despondent. God has been relegated to a genie whose job is to grant whatever people ask. I must inform you that God is yet sovereign and some things will not happen until it is time. I must seriously advice those who are impatient to take some lessons on how to be patient and wait on God. No promise, no matter how great, can be accessed and experienced without patience.

> *Hebrews 10:36* says, **"For ye have need of patience, that, after ye have done the will of God, ye might receive the promise."**

> The Amplified Bible says, **"For ye have need of steadfast patience and endurance, so that you may perform and fully accomplish the will of God, and thus receive and carry away [and enjoy to the full] what is promised."**

The same Greek word ***hupomone*** is used which, once again, describes having a cheerful endurance and constancy. We need a cheerful endurance with constancy and steadfast patience in order for us to fully accomplish the will of God and completely enjoy everything He promised.

FAITH – HOPE CONNECTION

There is a symbiotic relationship that exists between faith and hope. They actually work together and need each other to be successful. Let's look again at Hebrews 11:1 and extract the necessary principals from these two great truths.

> *Hebrews 11:1* **"Now faith is the substance of things hoped for, the evidence of things not seen."**

> The Amplified Bible says, **"Now faith is the assurance (the confirmation, the title deed) of the things [we] hope for, being the proof of things [we] do not see and the conviction of their reality [faith perceiving as real fact what is not revealed to the senses]."**

As we dissect the text defining the key words from their Greek derivatives, it looks something like this: Now **faith** [a credence, conviction of religious truth of God] is the **substance** [a setting under (support) concrete essence, assurance, confidence], of things **hoped for** [expected or have confidence in, trusting for], and the **evidence** [proof, conviction of things not seen] (invisible).

Faith provides the [conviction or convincing] which is the substance [support and essence] of hope [expectation or confidence]. And faith [conviction or convincing] is the evidence [proof, conviction of things not seen]. Please see chapter five for the full Greek breakdown of the text. *Faith actually supports what we expect and provides proof of its reality through our conviction which makes it a reality in our hearts before physical or material manifestation.*

SIX BINDING PRINCIPLES OF FAITH AND HOPE TOGETHER

1. **Faith provides the support, brace, under-propping, and foundation for hope.** This support is provided through assurance that comes from what faith is — *pistis* [a conviction of religious truth concerning God]. In other words, faith provides an inner convincing which is an inner *knowing* that God is sovereign and shall produce what hope is expecting.
2. **Hope must furnish something for faith to support and assure.** When people lose hope, they lose positive expectations which don't give faith anything to do. Usually when you find hopeless people, they are faithless also because faith is employed to provide conviction, support, and certify the inward evidence for hope. When hope is depleted, so is faith.
3. **Without hope there is nothing for faith to empower into reality.** Faith is what connects us to divinity and the power God possesses. When there is no hope or expectation, then faith has nothing which is expected or desired to bring into reality. Depression, sadness, sorrow, unbelief, fear, etc. are all enemies of hope and must be managed.

4. **Faith works to make what you hope for a reality.** Hope is what you desire. Faith is what brings that desire into reality. Because faith is invisible like hope, it is birthed in the spirit and shared in the thought realm of man. Therefore faith creates and possesses the evidence of hope before it materializes. Faith is a necessary currency of exchange to access God and do business within the kingdom. So then faith accesses the supernatural in order to release the supernatural to make visible the tangible reality that hope expected and faith orchestrated.
5. **The greater the hope, the greater the faith required to bring it into manifestation.** The bigger the dream and vision the more faith it takes to believe God for manifestation. God usually provides us with His vision which is much greater than what we ourselves alone can produce. God-sized vision inspires great hope within the spirit and mind of man. This produces a great imagination. A great imagination stretches beyond the boundaries of the natural and entertains the possibilities of the supernatural.
6. **Faith sets the stage for the supernatural.** Mark wonderfully pens the personal account of a woman who had an issue of blood for 12 years in *Mark 5:25-34*. Her story has been told around the world in multiple languages. Although there are many principles that can be extracted from her life, I only want to focus on a few. Mark records in *Mark 5:28,* **"For she said, If I may touch but his clothes, I shall be whole."** She spoke what she believed! It is apparent that this woman had been speaking inwardly and outwardly, "If I may touch just his clothes, I shall be made whole." She hoped or expected healing to come from Jesus despite her medical diagnosis. She spoke faith continually and expected healing before she came to Jesus.

Our mouths should always speak what we believe. The mouth is a mechanism that releases faith. Before she got to Jesus, she had already spoke and confessed her healing. The tongue is a mechanism that acts as the paint brush of our life and paints the most beautiful picture on the landscape of time and eternity. Faith had already been spoken and as her hand made a point of contact with his garment, she was healed and made whole. Faith pulled healing (virtue) power out of Jesus like a bucket draws water from a well.

KEEP YOUR HOPE ALIVE

The woman with the issue of blood didn't allow fear, negativity and doubt to steal her hope and faith. We must focus our spiritual and emotional energy on remaining positive no matter what. I make no apologies for saying that David is one of my favorite Bible personalities. He lives a life that is as much human as divinely inspired.

I can relate to David's triumphs and failures. His life reads like a chapter from a book on human behavior. He loves God, but he is also incredibly flawed and at times overcome by his passions. I must admit I can relate to David because he loved God, but yet struggled in life like you and I.

David allows us glimpses of his psychological state in **Psalms 42:5, "Why art thou cast down, O my soul? and why art thou disquieted in me? hope thou in God: for I shall yet praise him for the help of his countenance."** It is apparent that David is struggling with depression and turmoil. The word disquieted comes from the Hebrew word *hamah* which means *to make a loud sound, to be in great commotion or tumult, to rage, to be in an uproar.* David's heart and mind were in such tumult until he was moved to shout with a loud voice. I must admit I can relate. Sometimes the pressure from bills, family problems, poor physical health, disappointment, rejection, etc. can become so great until it feels like your head will explode. Have you ever had to release some steam through a good yell or loud scream? Real problems can put you in the pressure cooker and attempt to burn the very life out of you.

David understands the problem and immediately prescribes the remedy by saying, "hope thou in God." Anyone who is convinced of the existence of God and have a good understanding of who He is can identify with what David suggests. True hope can't be put in a man or woman. Ultimately people will fail you even on their best day, but God in His omnipotence cannot fail. Once we understand that God has a plan and that He has our best interest at heart, we can truly rest in knowing that even when bad things happen, His plan will ensure a wonderful future.

Jeremiah 29:11 says, **"For I know the thoughts that I think toward you, saith the LORD, thoughts of peace, and not of evil, to give you an expected end."**

The Amplified Bible says, **"For I know the thoughts and plans that I have for you, says the Lord, thoughts and plans for welfare and peace and not for evil, to give you hope in your final outcome."**

God's intentions for us despite disappointment, pain, trials, tribulations, and death are for us to have peace. If we have faith in God's divine providence and infinite love, then we can be secure in knowing that He is trustworthy and worthy of our faith. Therefore we can't allow our hope to become depleted because of adversity and hardships.

Difficult, damaging experiences can ultimately affect the way we view life and cripple our hope. We must fight to trust and have hope in God regardless of what opposes us. *Psalms 71:14* says, **"But I will hope continually, and will yet praise thee more and more."** Hope is a continual companion. Regardless of what stage of life you live in now, you must maintain hope. Young people hope for bright futures replete with a wonderful spouse, nice home, good job, great family, and incredible retirement. And the elderly who are retired look to enjoy their retirement years with family and friends as they prepare for a peaceful end on the latter side of life anticipating a new beginning on the other side in Heaven. We must always hope for something better.

David decided that he would always hope in God and that he would offer up praise to Him. We must learn how to be thankful for what we have — even the little things. I am sure that someone is reading this book and struggling in the most abhorrent ways. Don't allow your struggles to define you. You define your struggles. Open your heart and mouth unto God and release a praise that everyone, including your enemies, can hear. We must learn how to find good even on the most evil day of our life. Celebrate minor accomplishments as if they were major. Fill your heart daily with thanksgiving and don't let circumstances manipulate you.

Make a decision now that you will renew your spiritual and psychological filter. Regardless of how negative your past experiences have been, make a conscious choice to start living life through positive lenses. Don't allow pessimism or negativity to interpret your reality. You don't have to be a victim of past, flawed thinking and dead faith. Your life can change right now with a renewed commitment to God and by embracing the incredible empowered person He has ordained you to be. Yes, you do have a choice and having a choice gives you power!

YOU HAVE THE POWER TO CHOOSE HOPE AND FAITH OR PESSIMISM AND DOUBT. THE CHOICE IS UP TO YOU!

PERSONAL REFELCTIONS

Please feel free to discuss these questions with friends, family or a small group. Search yourself with an open heart and let God fill your every need and desire.

1. What does hope provide for you?
2. When hope is lost, how can it affect you and others?
3. Have you ever experienced depression? If so, when?
4. What does hope provide for the human race?
5. Romans 8:24-25 describes how hope is invisible. What points did the author make about this Scripture that enlightened you about hope?
6. What should your attitude be like when you are waiting for something?
7. Rehearse and discuss with a friend the six binding principles of faith and hope?
8. How important is your mouth or what you say in faith?
9. How did the woman with the issue of blood keep hope alive? How did David?
10. When is the last time you used praise as a weapon to fight back and help restore hope?

INTIMATE REFLECTIONS

As anchors are to ships, so is hope to the human race. Hope provides stability and prevents us from drifting aimlessly. Depression is like a faith-hope eating disease. It gnaws on the very strands and fibers of faith and hope leaving man adrift upon a sea of despair, hopelessness, and even suicide. Depression brings darkness that seeks to douse the light of optimism. Find Scriptures that will nourish and strengthen your faith and hope. Always remember the binding principles of hope and faith together and live by them. Don't allow your life to drift without a compass or destination. Drop your anchor of hope in the sea of life and rest knowing that no contrary wind can destroy your destiny when faith and hope are on board.

REFLECTIONS JOURNAL

Chapter 9

THE FAITH - POWER CONNECTION

...According to your faith be it unto you. Mark 9:29

I caution people to understand the Bible is not a book of magical spells, potions, and incantations. It is not a book to be utilized to wield power against a human enemy or control people. The Bible is the Word of God and is inspired to impart knowledge and wisdom and to empower believers to fulfill God's will in the earth. Many people want to take the principles of God's word and use them strictly for gain.

SEEK THE GIVER AND NOT THE GIFT

Our ability to use God's Word is based on our relationship with Him. It is through our relationship with Him and being filled with the Holy Spirit that we begin to use His power according to His will. We shouldn't expect to have God's power without first establishing a relationship with Him. I hear people saying, "I want to be anointed. I am praying for a greater anointing." It is good to want more of God's anointing. Actually, asking God to anoint you is not a bad prayer, but seek the Creator first.

When I say seek the Creator, I don't mean seek His anointing. Seek God with your heart. The power and anointing of God cannot be separated from God the person. You should want an intimate relationship with God more than anything. The Lord shared this revelation with me one day. I have prayed for years for a better relationship with God, but I emphasized requesting the anointing in my prayers more intensely than just seeking God. He shared with me that it is better to seek Him because of who He is and not just for what He can do. It is while loving Him and abiding in His presence that the very essence of God's Spirit emanates from Him and is imparted into us. In a practical life situation, as we spend more time with an individual, we get to know their ways, pick up some of their sayings, and partake of their spirit.

To constantly be in the presence of someone places one in a position for the exchange of both positive and negative things. Sometimes our speech changes, our style of dress, or even our thinking changes because of whom we associate with. **Proverbs 13:20 "He that walketh with wise men shall be wise but a companion of fools shall be destroyed."** The Amplified Bible says, **"He who walks [as a companion] with wise men is wise, but he who associates with [self confident] fools is [a fool himself and] shall smart for it.** Associations have a powerful affect on people. We are molded and shaped through associations for either good or bad. The power of association can either help or hurt you. Positive associations can bring about positive results and negative associations will bring negative results.

When you deal with positive people, you receive positive words, spirit, and life from them. When you deal with negative people, you receive negative words, spirit, and death. (John 6:63)

It is no coincidence that in the animal kingdom dogs associate with dogs, lions with lions, and rats with rats. We are usually drawn to people because they share basic similarities in terms of our likes and dislikes. These similarities enable us to relate better and focus on what we have in common. We tend to feel more comfortable around people who share our same opinions, perceptions, goals, likes, and dislikes. We literally feed and receive from those in whom we associate. If you want to be a dog, you have to run with dogs. If you want to be a buzzard, start flying with the buzzards. But if you want to be an eagle, you have got to nest, feed, fly, and fellowship with eagles. It is fascinating to see people change when they start associating and assimilating with a particular group. Some married couples that have been together a certain length of time look like sisters and brothers. ***The best associations make us better; the worst associations make us worse.***

Associating with God and allowing Him to fertilize the seed He implanted within you will cause you to become more like Him. Fellowship with the Father breeds intimacy that takes man into the inner depths of God and beyond the veil of superficiality. We begin to trust the Father and He allows us to prove our trustworthiness to Him. Trust in a relationship moves boundaries, restrictions, and inhibitions. When relationships have trust, those involved feel the freedom to expose oneself or become vulnerable and allow exchange on uninhibited levels. Trusting relationships are filled heavily with the substance of responsibility. Each trusts the other with being responsible for their heart, possessions, etc. Most people freely give their precious possessions to people they love and trust. God will freely give Himself to those whom He trusts. ***Psalms 25:14* "The secret of the Lord is with them that fear him and he will show them his covenant."**

The anointing or power of God is not to be entrusted with just anyone.

1) **You must have committed your heart to Jesus Christ as Lord and Savior.**
2) **You must seek and receive the promise of the Father which is the baptism of the Holy Ghost according to *Acts1:8; 2:4*.**
3) **Seek God with your whole heart.**
4) **Cultivate your personal relationship with God.**
5) **Start walking in the power of God daily.**

FAITH IS DIRECTLY CONNECTED TO GOD'S POWER

The thread that connects mankind to his Creator is faith. Our relationship with God is based on faith. The concept of faith is not foreign to most - just misunderstood. Many believers understand the necessity of faith and how pertinent it is to their lives on their quest to embrace God and utilize the authority He has given us. We recognize the need for faith, the reason for faith, and the power of faith. Yet we don't understand how faith is directly related to the Power Source and causes those things we believe for to translate into visible, touchable manifestations. In other words faith is power itself, but how does it relate to the power of God that actually converts what we believe into what we receive?

Have you ever heard a dynamic testimony of how God gave someone a car or somebody was handed the keys to a brand new house with no strings attached? Upon hearing these testimonies, it stirred your faith. Since you had a need similar to the one who testified, you said, "Yes, I am going to try that!" And you did, but you didn't get the same results. Have you ever wondered why? I am not claiming to have all the answers, nor am I attempting to list all of the factors involved that could have caused you to fail in receiving what you asked for. You do need to know that God has created you with a capacity to store and release His power at will.

Again I emphasize that sometimes there are other factors such as violating God's will, asking for lustful purposes, and more that can hinder you from receiving an answer to prayer. However, most people don't receive results because they don't possess enough power to produce what they say or ask for.

GOD'S POWER IS IN YOU

Let's consider *Ephesians 3:20*. It says, **"Now unto him that is able to do exceeding abundantly above all that we ask or think according to the power that worketh in us."** Now unto Him (God) that is able to do **exceeding** *(huper)* over, above, beyond abundantly above all that we **ask** *(aiteo)* beg, call for, crave or **think** *(noieo)* to exercise the mind, to comprehend, heed, consider, perceive, think, understand according to the **power** *(dunamis)* forcer, miraculous power that **worketh** *(energeo)* to be active, do, be mighty in us.

Paraphrasing, *"Now unto him that is able to do over, above, or beyond abundantly above what we ask, beg, call for, crave or comprehend, consider, perceive, think or understand according to the force of miraculous power that is active and mighty in us."* We usually remember that God can do anything, but we omit to acknowledge that what we need will be produced by what is within us through the possession of the Holy Spirit which is our inner power source.

In the field of electronics a capacitor is a component that stores power and releases or discharges it as needed in the electrical cycle of the circuit in which it is apart of. We have the capacity to harness God's power as well as release it when it is necessary. Most people acknowledge that through the Holy Spirit man has delegated power, but many are confused about when man should use this power and when God will personally intervene.

Here is an example. How many times have you heard the preacher say that the battle is not yours; it's the Lord's? Many have said that God will fight for you. How many times have you heard the same preacher or another one say, "God gave you power to tread on serpents and over all the power of the enemy and it is time for you to use your God-given power and fight your enemy."? I admit it sounds confusing. One is telling you to let God fight and the other is telling you to fight. Which one is it? Without spending too much time elaborating on statements, dispensations and context in which the statements were made, I will say the New Testament believer walks in a covenant with God where the power of God dwells within and the believer has the right to use it when necessary. The statements may sound ambiguous, but they are really connected because God fights our battles through His Covenant Word and through the release of power from a source He has delegated power and authority to. Believers are a source He has delegated power and authority to.

AUTHORITY GIVES POWER

Jesus expounds on delegated power after the seventy that He appointed to go into the nearby cities returned with wonderful stories about the success of their mission. He says in ***Luke 10:19,*** **"Behold I give unto you power to tread on serpents and scorpions and over all the power of the enemy and nothing shall by any means hurt you."** The word "power" is from the Greek word *exousia* which means authority, jurisdiction, liberty, right and strength. The second time the word "power" is used refers to the enemy's power which is from the Greek word *dunamis* meaning strength, violence, mighty (wonderful) work. The believer has *exousia* (authority, jurisdiction, liberty, right and strength) over the enemy's *dunamis* (strength, violence, mighty work). ***We have power over the enemy's power.***

Yes, the enemy has power; but the power of the Holy Spirit in which we possess is greater than that of the enemy which is the devil and his demonic allies. We must never forget God's power is greater than the devil's. Jesus echoes more confirmations of delegated power in ***Mark 16:17-18,*** **"And these signs shall follow them that believe, In my name shall they cast out devils they shall speak with new tongues." They shall take up serpents and if they drink any deadly thing, it shall not hurt them, they shall lay hands on the sick and they shall recover."**

I want to briefly expound upon the word believe in ***Mark 16:17***. The word "believe" comes from the Greek word *pisteuo* which means to have faith, to entrust, commit to trust, or put in trust with. While it is true that every believer has access to God's power, not every one will believe they can use it in accordance with the Bible's depiction. I know for some of you this is a revelation concerning this text. We usually associate this passage with the category of believers in general and fail to realize that this also speaks about *the belief of believers.*

There are many believers who quote this verse as justification for utilizing and appropriating the power of God in situations of need, but many yet don't believe. When I say believe, I mean that they don't have faith, entrust, or put trust in the power of God to be literally exercised in the way in which the text describes. They believe He has saved them; but they don't believe in the signs, new tongues, the power to take up serpents, or the power to be immune to poison when used against them. Nor do they have faith to lay hands on the sick and expect them to recover. ***James 1:6-7*** says, **"But let** him ask in faith, nothing wavering. For he that wavereth is like a wave of the sea driven with the wind and tossed. For let not that man think that he shall receive anything of the Lord." It is possible to be a believer and ask in doubt and not receive what you ask for.

THE TRUE BELIEVER HAS POWER AND AUTHORITY

Just because you are a believer does not mean you are automatically exercising your rights and authority as a child of God. You must first believe that these rights and powers are available to you before you can use them. One can be born into privilege and power but act like a peasant. A young prince or princess will not consciously take advantage of his or her royal privileges until they recognize that they are positioned in a hierarchy which has bestowed inherent power upon them. It is because of a lack of faith that many of God's people die daily from sickness, disease, or tragedy.

Yes, the enemy is launching his attacks against us, but how many believe that the power they possess is actually greater than the enemy's? So what usually happens is they die as believers in God but not as a believer in divine healing. Some even believe in divine healing but not for their situation. It is usually easier to believe and pray for someone else than it is for us to pray and believe God for ourselves. Signs will follow those who believe, have faith, commit to trust, and put trust in God.

Prior to Christ's ascension it is recorded in *Acts 1:8,* **"Ye shall receive power after that the Holy Ghost is come upon you and ye shall be witnesses unto me both in Jerusalem and in all Judea and in Samaria and unto the uttermost part of the earth."** The word "power" in that verse is the same Greek word *dunamis* used to describe the enemy's power in *Luke 10:19*. It means strength, violence, might, wonderful work. After the Holy Ghost comes upon the believer, they receive God's strength and ability to wield violence against the enemy and do mighty, wonderful works. What awesome power God has shared with His people!

The scriptures I have mentioned supporting the believers authority are just a few among many that are contained within the

Bible. Let's look at these same verses in the Amplified Bible. *Luke 10:19* "Behold! I have given you authority and power to trample upon serpents and scorpions, and [physical and mental strength and ability] over all the power of that the enemy [possesses]; and nothing shall in any way harm you."

Mark 16:17-18 "And these attesting signs will accompany those who believe: in my name they shall drive out demons; they will speak in new languages; They will pick up serpents; and [even] if they drink anything deadly, it will not hurt them; they will lay their hands on the sick, and they will get well."

Acts 1:8 "But ye shall receive power (ability, efficiency, and might) when the Holy Spirit has come upon you, and you shall be My witnesses in Jerusalem and all Judea and Samaria and to the ends (the very bounds) of the earth."

The believer is positioned in the hierarchy of the Kingdom of God as a ruler who has power and authority. I believe the position of son and joint heir with Christ is just the beginning for believers. Believers must act within the jurisdiction and position of governance that they have been given.

One of the most powerful scriptures in the Bible that distinctly correlates thinking with being is *Proverbs 23:7A,* **"For as he thinketh in his heart, so is he."** Whatever is in the mind of man determines who man is. We are not greater or less than our thinking. We are a product of our thinking. Our thinking is determined by several factors - genetics, environment, learned behavior, spiritual instruction, and others. The thoughts that we have determine who we are. If we don't have faith to accept our God-given position and the power that comes with it, we won't see the fruits of this position nor its' power.

PSYCHOLOGY AND THEOLOGY

Our theology and psychology has a direct impact on our thinking. It is virtually impossible to separate the connection of theology from psychology. Your study of God determines your belief in God which can only take place as it is absorbed within your psychology or the systemic processing of thought. Both theology and psychology have an affect on each other. You cannot think about God without your mind, but yet you cannot embrace God without theology. Psychology is responsible for your systematic processing of emotion and thought while theology is responsible for your systematic processing of God into understandable concepts. Bad thinking can produce bad theology and bad theology can produce bad thinking.

The transformation of the mind occurs with the infiltration of theology into the core of one's spirit and psyche. ***Romans 12:2* "And be not conformed to this world but be ye transformed by the renewing of your mind, that ye may be able to prove what is that good and acceptable and perfect will of God."** The word "transformed" comes from the Greek word *metamorphoo* which means to transform, change, transfigure. The word "transform" means to change the form or appearance of. Transformation is the process of the mind being changed into another mind. Your old mind is changed into a new mind. You are transformed by the renewing of your mind. The word "renewing" comes from the Greek word *anakainosis* which means renovations, renewing. The word "renovations" means *to make fresh or sound again, as though new, cleanup, replace worn parts in repair, or rebuild.*

Transformation of the mind occurs when the mind is made fresh or new and old parts are replaced. ***Titus 3:5* "Not by works of righteousness which we have done, but according to his mercy he saved us, by the washing of regeneration, and renewing of the Holy Ghost."** We must feed on the Word of God in order to continue to supply ourselves with the nourishment for transformation of spirit and mind. It is the ingestion and digestion of God's Word into our spirit that radically transforms the mind. The absorption of Scripture and the extraction of divine life from Scripture produce divine thinking and divine manifestation in the believer.

Matthew 4:4 states, **"But he answered and said It is written man shall not live by bread alone but by every word that proceedeth out of the mouth of God."** The word used for "word" in this text comes from the Greek word *rhema* which is a spoken, fresh, specific word from God. The child of God lives by feeding on and living by the Word of God. Jesus says in ***John 6:63b,*** **"the words that I speak unto you, they are spirit, and they are life."** His words are spirit *(pneuma)* and life *(zoe)*. God's Word contains His essence and life that is supernatural. Therefore our spiritual life and transformed thinking is dependant upon a healthy, sumptuous, gourmet meal of the Word of God.

The shaping and molding factors of life help to form our theology and psychology. We must believe in our heart that we are joint heirs and co-rulers with God. We must believe that according to the power of the Holy Ghost within we have jurisdiction over Satan and worldly things. If we don't believe it, we won't live it. If we don't live it, we won't walk in it. If we don't walk in it, we won't exercise it. Therefore as Jesus says in ***Matthew 9:29*** **"According to your faith so be it unto you."** What you think is connected with what you believe which is connected with what you do which defines who you are. If you think faith, you will be a person of faith; but if you think doubt, you will be a person of doubt. If you have the faith to believe, you have the faith to receive. Negativity breeds negativity. Negative people get negative results because of negative thinking and speaking. In mathematics a minus plus a minus equals a minus. We can't expect to be positive when we are filled with minuses.

If you have a warped, twisted, inferior opinion of your position and place in God, then you are living as a warped, twisted inferior person. Believers must believe in signs and wonders before they can personally speak and pray them into manifestation.

BELIEVERS MUST REALLY BELIEVE

I have been blessed over the years to see the power of God manifested through healing, miracles, deliverance, etc. As a pastor's son, I have seen the supernatural power of God perform many wonders. My father, Bishop Charlie Green Jr., believed in the demonstration of the power of God. Although I am currently Non-Denominational, my roots stem from the Pentecostal branches of The Church of God in Christ Inc. I have the utmost respect for the organization that helped birth, train, and nurture me. We were taught to believe in the gifts of the Spirit and the manifestations of the power of God years before other organizations embraced it. We believed *James 5:15* which said, **"And the prayer of faith shall save the sick, and the Lord shall raise him up; and if he have committed sins, they shall be forgiven him."**

I have many vivid memories of God's power in action, but two incidents really stick out in my mind. During one of the Sunday morning worship services an older member became ill. She literally died in church. Many people who are familiar with death realize that you lose control of all bodily functions. As a result, whatever is within your bladder or bowels is excreted into your clothing. That sweet mother of the church died while in the service. She slumped over, lost her bodily fluids, and had no pulse. One of the members immediately noticed it and notified my father who was sitting in the pulpit. He immediately rushed to her side with the aid of the clergy and saints. He laid hands on her and began to rebuke death in the name of Jesus. He prayed with the assistance of the saints and within minutes she began to breathe again and life returned into her body. The woman lived several months after that incident.

Another incident happened many years after the aforementioned one when I was a young adult in the ministry. Our oldest member in the church died while sitting on the pew in Sunday morning worship service. The same scenario happened. This time an RN who was a member of the church checked the pulse and heart beat and there was none. This mother also lost control of her bodily fluids. My father was notified again and this time I was at his side along with other members of the church. He led the prayer and began to call on the name of God. He again rebuked death in the name of Jesus and life returned into the precious mother. The woman lived several years after this incident also.

NEVER UNDERESTIMATE THE POWER OF FAITH

I have been blessed to have several personal testimonies of praying for people and God restored their health and some their lives. About one year before the first version of this book was published, God allowed me to become connected to a precious woman of God named Marguerite Swan. This wonderful, sweet woman knew my grandfather, the late Elder Charlie Green Sr., and my father, Bishop Charlie Green Jr. The Lord gave me favor with her and she developed the same kind of respect for me that she held for both my grandfather and father. She was a beautiful woman of God. One night while sleeping, the Lord revealed to me in three successive dreams that she was going to die. I literally saw her Home-Going service in the dreams.

I was troubled about what I saw and when I awoke I began to pray for her. Later that same morning the Lord spoke to me and said He wanted me to go and pray for her. I was somewhat reluctant and began to push it to the back of my mind. The Lord spoke to me a second time and I experienced what felt like a nudging in my back. This time He said, *"I told you to go and pray for her!"*

I immediately got on the phone and called a church member who made arrangements for me to offer prayer. I went over to Mother Swan's house at 6 p.m. on a Tuesday evening. Her daughter, Helen Baker a woman of God in her own right, was there with us and we talked for a while. I enjoyed the fellowship with her and just like the precious saints of old who loved God with all their heart, she was full of the joy of the Lord and testified of His mighty power. When the time was right, I began to focus on the reason why I was there. I didn't reveal what I saw in the dream, but I let her know I was there on assignment from God. The three of us prayed. I prayed the prayer of protection and covering and I rebuked death.

After the prayer, we embraced each other and I left to go to a service at my church. When I got in the car, I immediately started talking to God. I said, *"Lord just as sure as my name is what it is, something is getting ready to happen to this woman."* I reminded the Lord that this was a woman of God who belonged to Him. I also asked, *"Lord, because I was obedient and did what You told me to do, spare her life and give her an extension. Lord, I did what You said. If You don't do it for anyone else, do it for me."* While I was praying, the presence of God began to shower down on me in the vehicle. I prayed and praised God all the way to church.

The next day on Wednesday I went out of town. While I was traveling, I received a phone call sometime in the evening. A member of our church who is also a close friend notified me that Mother Swan died and the doctors were working on her. Twenty-four hours hadn't passed since I had left her house. Needless to say, I wasn't surprised. But I didn't think it was over. I later received a report that the doctors thought she wasn't going to make it. They had made several attempts to revive her, but she wasn't responding. Then all of a sudden she started breathing again and even the doctors were amazed.

The Lord spoke to me afterwards and reminded me of how He stopped by and had a conversation with Abraham concerning Sodom and Gomorrah, a place in which his nephew Lot lived. He spoke something to me which one of her children later came to me and said. He said that if I hadn't prayed for her, she would have died and not come back. In all my past experiences in seeing God work, this situation disturbed me greatly. How could God trust me with such a responsibility? What if I had disobeyed? While I was grateful God used me as an instrument, I was also humbled. Only God can get the glory from something like this.

Mother Swan lived six more months and then passed away. Her family says that after God brought her back, she was never the same. Her message was, **"It Is All About God!"** In those final months she spent time with her children and continued to do God's work with greater passion until He called her home.

What if I had doubted God's power? What if I didn't believe God could cover and protect with His awesome power? What if I doubted my position in God? In order to be effective in walking and seeing Kingdom principles manifested and produce power, faith is a must and there is no room for wavering or doubt. Faith is the connection to God's power. As believers, we must believe in order to receive the manifestations of the power of God. We must walk in a place in God where the Word of God has convinced us of who we are in Him. Knowing who we are in Him moves us into the realm of faith and gives us access to the power of God.

PERSONAL REFLECTIONS

Please feel free to discuss these questions with friends, family or a small group. Search yourself with an open heart and let God fill your every need and desire.

1. What does the author say about a relationship with God and the Anointing?
2. Proverbs 13:20 speaks of associations. Our associations will either make us better or worse. Who are you associating with? Do you need to reevaluate your associations?
3. Ephesians 3:20 tells us that believers have power (***dunamis***) working within us. What does ***dunamis*** mean in this verse? How do you know if the power is working within you?
4. We have authority over the enemy according to Mark 16:17-18. But frankly, some Christians don't believe God will do certain things. Can the unbelief of Christians affect their ability to receive? Do you know of any Christians, organizations, and denominations that don't believe certain things the Bible says? If so, what do they not believe?
5. Does psychology and theology have an effect on each other? How?
6. How important is mind transformation to any Christian? How does mind transformation have an impact on your faith? Do you feel that your faith is getting stronger?
7. The author mentioned some miracles that he has seen over the years. Do you believe in miracles? Have you witnessed any miracles? If so, what?

INTIMATE REFLECTIONS

Building a relationship with God is one of the most important things you can do. To know Him is to know your Creator. Remember believers possess power and authority over any circumstances including our enemies. Embrace your God-given position and believe that the supernatural power of God is available to you. Let this knowledge transform your mind and it will increase your faith which will change your life. Fill your circle of life with people who have great faith and disconnect yourself from limited, small-minded believers. I can tell a lot about who you are by the people you closely associate with. Who is in your circle?

REFLECTIONS JOURNAL

Chapter 10

IF AT FIRST YOU DON'T SUCCEED

…help thou mine unbelief. Mark 9:24

It was a normal day in our household. The children were playing, my wife had finished her work day, and I had transferred my work from the church office to my home office. In an attempt to please my taste buds, my wife decided to try and surprise me by making a dish I had grown to love over the years - chicken and dumplings.

Vanissa moved about in the kitchen gathering her ingredients and selecting her utensils to prepare the meal. Since she had never prepared chicken and dumplings, she enlisted the services of one of the master cooks in our family namely Aunt Dorothy. This Aunt was one of the best and had years of professional and domestic cooking experience. The instructional session was done via telephone. Vanissa was now pumped, primed, and ready to set out on her culinary journey.

As she went about the kitchen, she mentally reviewed all the pointers she had been given by Aunt Dorothy to prepare the meal to the best of her ability. She slowly followed each step and added all the necessary ingredients. I went into the kitchen to check on her progress as I periodically do. Sometimes while she is trying to cook or clean, I hug and squeeze on her. So it is no strange thing for me to be present briefly while she is preparing our meals. By this time the secret dish of chicken and dumplings was in the pot boiling.

When I inquired as to how the meal was progressing, she was simultaneously checking the chicken and dumplings. Her next reply was, "It's not turning out right. It's sticking." She then told me she was attempting to make me chicken and dumplings. She inserted a large spoon into the pot to stir and realized the dumplings had burned and were sticking to the bottom of the pot. Her attempt to make chicken and dumplings had failed. To her regret, we had to eat something else for dinner that night. Rest assured she is going to try again.

FAILURE IS A PART OF GROWTH

I am sure that you probably know or have many stories of failures in attempting to cook or perform some task outside of the realm of your expertise. The simple fact of the matter is that sometimes even with the best instructions we try and fail. Trial and error is a part of life, especially when you are walking with God. I will be the first one to admit I have made many mistakes and expect to make more. I believe the body of Christ excessively ridicules the failures of people and this is not advantageous for the body at large. Sanctification and salvation are progressive and so is spiritual growth. ***2 Corinthians 1:10* "Who delivered us from so great a death, and doth deliver: in whom we trust that he will yet deliver us."** The verse gives three tenses: *delivered* refers to the past, *doth deliver* refer to the present, and *yet deliver* refers to the future.

We focus on the instantaneous but not the progressive. Our walk with God occurs in stages of progression. We advance spiritually in steps, stages, and phases. The Bible succinctly declares, **"But we all, with open face beholding as in a glass the glory of the Lord, are changed into the same image from glory to glory, even as by the Spirit of the Lord."** *2 Corinthians 3:18*

Our metamorphosis or change occurs from glory to glory, level to level, height to height, depth to depth, and faith to faith. Since our journey is a process of progressions, we see, understand, and know only in part. We don't have the benefit of knowing everything in our phases of development. So we make decisions and execute our daily functions accordingly. This literally means without divine inspiration we make decisions from partial, limited knowledge, understanding, and insight. Your current ability to make decisions is based upon what you have already learned and experienced.

Sometimes the aforementioned qualifications are good enough to help us make the best decisions, but at other times it isn't. The time that it is insufficient is usually because the banks of information in which we possess are limited and incapable of providing adequate answers. As we progress and gain more information through learning and experience, we are better prepared to make future decisions. We grow from being a novice to an experienced veteran.

THE TRUTH IS SOMETIMES YOU FAIL

Trying to utilize the principles of faith doesn't guarantee success. Many will attempt to have faith and will fail miserably. Many will try to follow the recipe of the pastor, Bible, etc. and will at sometime still fail. It is true that we attempt to explain faith, preach on it, criticize people for lacking it, and encourage using it. However we usually don't inform them that if you fail, don't stop. Try it again. I am by no means using this chapter to enumerate the reasons why people fail to have faith. The truth of the matter is that the principle or law of faith is flawless; but people are flawed and our application of these principles is usually flawed. Therein lay the problem.

To discuss the myriad of misapplications and misappropriations of Scripture and theology would take several pages. I merely want to speak to you truthfully and realistically because I know many have tried and failed in using faith. I know personally I have tried many times in the past and failed miserably. I have believed for ministry success, homes, cars, finances, spiritual matters, etc. and received nothing. Again the Law of Faith works, but there are factors in which believers have to line up with to see manifested what they have requested. Some who have tried and failed feel like weaklings, freaks, or outcasts. They don't realize they are in a great company of Biblical patriarchs who I call faith-figures and at times struggled and failed in having faith.

I am reminded of Abraham as he traveled through Gerar between Kadesh and Shur. He encountered a situation that caused his faith to fail. (Genesis 20) Abraham and his family were traveling through a strange territory called Gerar on their way to the land of promise. It was common in those days for Kings and strangers to take women from travelers to be their concubines. Resistance to these demands could bring death. Since Abraham was unsure of his fate as a stranger in Gerar, he told what some call a "half-lie" - but really there is no such thing.

Yes, Sarah was his half-sister but she also was his wife. Although Abraham lived in a dispensation when God had not instituted a law against lying, he nonetheless shouldn't have done it. Abraham feared they would kill him and take his wife. So he told Abimelech that Sarah was his sister. Just as Abraham feared, Abimelech took Sarah and intended to make her his wife.

What? Abraham - a man of faith, the father of faith. How could this be? What happened to his faith? Could it be that his faith failed? The story of him waiting twenty-five years for a promised seed is preached on frequently; but what about his challenges and failures in trying to have faith before the seed of promise had manifested? Like many of us, Abraham received a Word from God and stepped out in faith, but this time the faith he had failed because he lied to save his life. Yes, he attempted to deceive Abimelech just to save his life!

GOD ALWAYS HAS A PLAN TO OVERCOME OUR FAILURES

It took God to speak up for Abraham to help get him out of the mess he was in. ***Genesis 20:2-7* And Abraham said of Sarah his wife, She is my sister: and Abimelech king of Gerar sent, and took Sarah. But God came to Abimelech in a dream by night, and said to him, Behold, thou art but a dead man, for the woman which thou hast taken; for she is a man's wife. But Abimelech had not come near her: and he said, Lord, wilt thou slay also a righteous nation? Said he not unto me, She is my sister? and she, even she herself said, He is my brother: in the integrity of my heart**

and innocency of my hands have I done this. And God said unto him in a dream, Yea, I know that thou didst this in the integrity of thy heart; for I also withheld thee from sinning against me: therefore suffered I thee not to touch her. Now therefore restore the man his wife; for he is a prophet, and he shall pray for thee, and thou shalt live: and if thou restore her not, know thou that thou shalt surely die, thou, and all that are thine.

God spoke to Abimelech in a dream and threatened to kill him and every person he was connected to. As great as Abraham was, he was yet a man who was susceptible to failure. *Isaiah 46:10* says, **"Declaring the end from the beginning, and from ancient times the things that are not yet done, saying, My counsel shall stand, and I will do all my pleasure."** God has foreknowledge. He knew the end from the beginning. He knows everything before it happens. His knowledge is vast and endless. He definitely knew what Abraham was going to say to Abimelech before he said it. God didn't allow Abraham's error to sabotage his destiny. He simply pre-planned a way for Abraham to escape with his life and wife in tact.

The truth of the matter is this: God has already accounted for our weaknesses, errors, and mistakes. As long as we are willing to repent and move forward, He will continue to provide and push us toward our destiny. Abraham's failure didn't forfeit the blessing and our failures won't either. God already has a plan to navigate through our distrust, doubt, weaknesses, and personal failings. Since God first called upon man to trust Him, He has patiently and graciously forgiven us many times despite our imperfections. The list of imperfect characters is long. It spans from Adam to the disciples to modern day Christians. While we have the greatest amount of respect for all of the men and women mentioned in Scripture, they were all imperfect. Jesus Christ hand-picked twelve and every last one had a flaw. And although they walked with Him, they yet struggled to believe what He said.

Yes, failure in using faith was common among the twelve disciples who followed Christ. The twelve that followed Jesus had seen Him work many miracles; but when it counted, they didn't have faith. One such occasion was in *Matthew 8:24-27* when fear came upon the disciples as they were out at sea and it appeared they were going to perish. *The disciples had more faith in the tempestuous waves to destroy them than in the power of Jesus to save them.* Jesus arose and rebuked the winds and then He turned and rebuked the disciples saying, **"O Ye of little faith."** If that wasn't failure, I don't know what is! Their inability to have faith in Jesus in that moment didn't disqualify them from service or greatness. As you keep reading the book of Acts and other New Testament books that many of them wrote, you will see that they became mighty men of God who literally turned the world upside down. Their past failures didn't abort God's destiny for them. Christians throughout the ages have been inspired to live by faith just from reading about the trials, tribulations, and supernatural works of the twelve disciples who later became Apostles.

SOMETIMES WE FAIL BEFORE WE SUCCEED

Yes, the disciples had many failures. They started out weak, but finished strong. They grew and matured eventually becoming the founding fathers of the first church. These men progressed from being cursing, weak, fighting, shallow men to becoming Holy, loving men of depth filled with faith and the power of God. The same Peter who acknowledged Christ as the Son of God eventually betrayed him three times during the trial. However that same Peter was renewed in hope after the resurrection and at Pentecost emerged as the leader.

He grew to become the first spokesman and ambassador for the church. He passionately writes in *1 Peter 1:16,* **"For we have not followed cunningly devised fables, when we made known unto you the power and coming of our Lord Jesus Christ, but were eyewitnesses of his majesty."** This verse proves that Peter grew from being an immature, rash follower who denied Christ to becoming a leader who boldly proclaimed His power and majesty.

It is important to know that it's alright you tried and failed, but that shouldn't be the end of the story. Abraham didn't quit because he experienced failure. He learned how to trust God and eventually became known as the friend of God. Peter didn't quit when he denied Christ three times. He humbled himself at the feet of Jesus after the resurrection and became a shining example of how persistence and determination will thrust you into the eternal pages of Scripture as one of God's great Apostles. While it is true that the law of faith is perfect, we aren't. Therefore we must strive to know what it takes to achieve optimal results in using faith. Our quest will take a lifetime, but it will yield eternity.

DELAY IS NOT ALWAYS DENIAL

During the course of writing this book I have seen God work many wonderful works; but I have also been personally challenged in my faith to exercise faith against all odds. I mentioned in a previous chapter concerning the challenge of purchasing the church facility in which we are currently worshipping. Many people don't know that the book in which you are reading now was a challenge to my faith.

My funds were very limited. I couldn't even afford to pay for the cost of self-publishing. I am virtually an unknown to most of the world. Many of you reading this book just became acquainted with me. No major publishing company knew me. No notable, well-known preacher or celebrity knew my name, but yet you are reading this book. This book was labor intensive and time consuming. From writing to printing took an extended amount of time, but yet you are reading this book. How would I market this book? How much would it cost to market it? Who would want to buy it? Most people didn't even know I existed, but yet you are reading this book! *I was challenged and even delayed, but not denied!*

Another major area of challenge was for a home. My wife and I moved into a home under certain pretenses that eventually fell through. We knew before we moved in our credit and financial portfolio wouldn't merit purchasing a house and certainly not the house we wanted. We were assured that this would not seriously interfere with the process. Prior to moving in, we lived in another city thirty miles south of the church in which I was pastor. We felt the unction to move and eventually found a house in the city where the church was located. The house had been taken off the market and was no longer for sale, but with God's favor they allowed us to move in.

We started with an original set of pretenses that soon changed and caused our journey to be a lengthy one which enlisted many mortgage companies, brokers, meetings, projected closing dates, unreasonable interest rate proposals, and endless documentation retrieval. Our pursuit led us into a wilderness of professionals who had many suggestions and opinions, but no solutions that would suit us. What was supposed to take up to three months took over two years. This great challenge attacked our faith and eventually led us to a place of indifference.

My wife and I found ourselves feeling scorned and rejected which led to us becoming unconcerned with the whole ordeal. We soon felt as if we would have to abandon the home. It seemed as if every effort we made to resolve this process was hopeless. During this time, we received numerous prophecies and even words of wisdom concerning other houses, but to no avail.

My wife and I regrouped and recommitted our faith to believe God for wherever He wanted us to live. In my conversations with God I reminded Him that this situation was not supposed to be predicated on our credit or financial status. It was about *Him*. (However I do advise people to build their credit ratings and be good stewards.) From that day forward indifference turned into anticipation. I began to eagerly anticipate through hope and define with faith the outcome of this situation. From that day forward I rested in the Lord.

I thank God for the co-owner of the home who is a sincere and genuine woman of God. Initially her role in the process was behind the scenes. But she soon stepped to the forefront of the proceedings and the complexion of the situation slowly began to change. She exercised love and patience throughout this ordeal. It was during my period of resting and relaxing in God that she encountered a woman who was a mortgage broker. She began to share our situation with the mortgage broker who immediately contacted us and offered her services. I must admit that when the broker called I was somewhat skeptical because we had been through multiple brokers with no success, but I felt to just go with the flow.

After two seemingly endless years, we closed on the house with miracle money at closing and financial terms that fit perfectly. In our season of waiting, our home appreciated in value. Had our financial situation really changed for the better? No, because when we started the process, my wife was working. So we had two incomes to work with. In the meantime, my wife left her job to come home and spend time with our young children. We went from two incomes to one and the process moved forward without resistance. The broker was amazed at the seamless and expeditious transaction. How can you go from struggling to get a house with two incomes, be reduced to one, still have the same financial challenges, but buy the home for the same price without the slightest hint of difficulty? *We were delayed, but not denied!*

When faith, patience, and hope are applied you can wait until destiny intersects with time and see the manifestation of your faith. There are sometimes when our fate is faith and we must wait. Then there are times God allows situations to fall apart to show that where man ends He begins. *He sometimes allows it to deteriorate to the lowest state so that when He fixes it, there will be no doubt in anyone's mind that **He** did it.* During your wait you must exercise faith and learn how to wait. You may be delayed but not denied!

The man with the son who was possessed with a deaf and dumb spirit as mentioned in Mark 9:24 vacillated between faith and doubt. He had watched his son deteriorate from docility to hostility. Evil spirits had confiscated his body. And like the puppet master controlled puppets with strings, so did these evil spirits control the young boy. The father watched in horror as the son was manipulated into suicidal excursions that compelled him to attempt to drown or burn himself to death. How hopeless and hapless the father felt, but thankfully hope would arise in the person of Jesus Christ.

The father heard and knew of His power, but was yet challenged with the nefarious reality of his son's seemingly incurable condition. He pleaded for the Master to heal him. When questioned about his faith, he valiantly answered affirmatively; but would soon sway back toward doubt because of past attempts that failed to cure his son. Even the apprentices of Jesus were powerless do deal with such contemptuous wickedness.

Despite the man's ambiguous answer, Jesus quickly exercised His authority by overpowering the evil spirits and banishing them from the body of the young boy. The Savior looked beyond the timid, double-mindedness of the father and with compassion put evil to shame. Our loving God is so empathetic to our plight that when we fail, He finds a way to help us succeed. Don't ponder too long over your failures because God is ready to forcibly remove all evil to bring you the greatest good. Trouble may be present but God is prepared to help you even in your darkest hour.

The days ahead will be challenging and filled with obstacles which are intent on destroying your desire to use faith. Take my advice: *Whatever you do, don't stop trying. Ask for help and get it! You have been armed with "Why Faith?" So use it to open new doors, experience the endless successful possibilities in life and become intimate with God in a way beyond your loftiest dreams.*

WHY FAITH? *"Your Guide to Surviving and Thriving in Tough Times"*

PERSONAL REFLECTIONS

Please feel free to discuss these questions with friends, family or a small group. Search yourself with an open heart and let God fill your every need and desire.

1. What do 2 Corinthians 1:10 and 2 Corinthians 3:8 discuss? How does this apply to you?
2. The author discusses Genesis chapter 20 which describes a portion of Abraham's life particularly when he failed. Can you relate to this story? Have you ever lied about something or used deception because you didn't trust God?
3. Have you ever failed a test like Abraham? What did you do after the failure? What did God do? Did it work out?
4. Have you ever seen God work miracles, but then doubt Him when a new crisis or storm arises? If so, why?
5. What is the author trying to convey in talking about failure and delay?
6. Have you ever failed in trying to believe God for something? If so, what?
7. What are you doing about your faith now? Are you more determined to succeed now? If so, why?

INTIMATE REFLECTIONS

No real winner wants to lose and most people hate to fail. Learning how to live by faith and trust in God isn't always easy. I have failed many times in walking with God and so have those who came before me. Sometimes we learn more about ourselves after we fail than when we succeed. We must know that at some time in our walk with God that we will try something and not get the results we desired. A real winner accepts failure as motivation and continues to compete until he conquers his goal. One thing is true. If you have ever failed, you are in good company. History records many great men and women who failed at something, but still persevered to win the prize. So what are you going to do about your latest failure?

WHY FAITH? "Your Guide to Surviving and Thriving in Tough Times"

REFLECTIONS JOURNAL

EPILOGUE

I hope that your journey through the pages of this book have been fulfilling, enlightening, and empowering. Many say that life is just a journey. I won't quibble with that statement. Faith is also a journey. As we navigate through life encountering the good, bad, and even troublesome winds of adversity we label as storms, we must exercise faith.

Our challenge is always reaching past the dimension of sight into the invisible. What we see and interpret visually and emotionally tend to impress upon us a stronger sense of reality. It is a part of our nature to believe that what we see is really our reality. In essence faith looks beyond tangible, physical, and sense-certified interpretations thus creating a reality of God-like proportions.

If you have strayed away from God, come back to Him. The key to having faith restored and eventually learning how to utilize it effectively is directly predicated upon your relationship with God. He is the author of faith and therefore must be the lifeline and tutor to instruct pupils on how to wield it.

It is obvious that we live in tough times and our faith is truly being tested and stretched in many ways. We must respond candidly, definitively, and decisively to whatever opposition challenges us. Face trouble like I faced dogs and bullies in my neighborhood. Look them square in the eye, show no fear, and be ready to stand your ground at all cost. Our stand must be one of faith, hope, and patience. Faith provides conviction, assurance, and evidence. Hope provides expectation, anticipation, and an object for faith to translate into spiritual and natural reality. Patience provides a right attitude of gratitude and a will of fortitude empowering us to wait with cheerfulness as long as it takes until the plan of God manifests before our natural eyes.

While failure is not an option, it is a reality. It happens! Real faith and hope will pick us up and propel us to the next challenge despite past failures. Sometimes we fail in trying to implement and execute certain divine principles. Our humanity at times replaces our divinity and we succumb to failure. It happens! Just because you fail doesn't mean that you have to reside in failure. It should be treated as a monument on the landscape of life that you passed on a road trip which is quickly fading into oblivion.

If you just experienced a failed mortgage, marriage, job, relationship, business transaction, or even depression, sadness, and despair, my word for you is GET UP!! Yes, God is all-powerful. You are extremely gifted. And yes, you have faith. No matter how small it may be, you have faith. Now tap into what faith brings and watch your world begin to change into something that glorifies God and empowers you with greatness. Faith will help you navigate and thrive in your storm. ***IF YOU CAN BELIEVE IT, YOU CAN RECEIVE IT!***

FAITH BUILDING TOOLS

1. LISTEN TO GOOD TEACHING AND PREACHING IN ORDER TO BUILD YOUR FAITH. *Romans 10:17* "**So then faith cometh by hearing, and hearing by the word of God.**" The Word of God is power, life, and transformative. The key to walking in faith after we are saved (born again) is to continue to make deposits of the Word of God in our heart and mind. Good teaching and preaching make rich deposits. Our thinking must be transformed so that we embrace God's thinking and ultimately His reality. There is a knowledge-faith connection. The more we know about God's Word, the more it inspires and increases our faith.

2. MEDITATE ON THE WORD OF GOD DAY AND NIGHT TO SOLIDIFY AND PURIFY YOUR FAITH. *Psalms 1:2-3* "**But his delight is in the law of the LORD; and in his law doth he meditate day and night. And he shall be like a tree planted by the rivers of water, that bringeth forth his fruit in his season; his leaf also shall not wither; and whatsoever he doeth shall prosper.**" The word "meditate" as used in the Old Testament doesn't just mean to rehearse in the mind or think on it. It also means to mutter, speak, or utter.

You should both speak and think the Word. Speaking makes the Word audible which is then caught by your hearing which in turn is processed by the mind. A cycle of speaking, hearing, and thinking is created. The newly created positive cycle changes your thinking which affects your faith and empowers your life. Meditation is a tool for transformation. We must believe and become what we read in the Bible.

3. SPEAK WITH YOUR MOUTH WHAT YOU BELIEVE IN YOUR HEART BECAUSE THE MOUTH CONFIRMS AND RELEASES FAITH. *Job 22:28* **"Thou shalt also decree a thing, and it shall be established unto thee: and the light shall shine upon thy ways."** *Proverbs 18:21* **"Death and life are in the power of the tongue: and they that love it shall eat the fruit thereof."** The mouth is the creative mechanism of mankind. It is an instrument, paint brush, and catalyst that release faith to access the supernatural and bring into existence what we say.

We have the supernatural DNA of God within us. God has given us His best example of how He uses speech in creating the world as recorded in the book of Genesis. He speaks what He wants and it comes into existence. Death and life are literally contained within what we say which are results of what we think and believe. We must choose to shape our world and align it with God's plan for our lives. Use your mouth to build up your life - not tear it down.

4. ASSOCIATE AND SURROUND YOURSELF WITH POSITIVE, FAITH-FILLED PEOPLE. *Psalms 119:63* **"I am a companion of all them that fear thee, and of them that keep thy precepts."** It is better to join yourself to people who share like faith and like passions as it pertains to life and Godliness. Words have power and if you spend time with people who misuse the power of words by speaking doom, gloom, and pessimism, it will impact your thinking. Words are also conditioning tools. Words have the power to build up or tear down, inflate or deflate, bring joy or sadness, kill or give life, and paint broad, light strokes of happiness or dark, narrow gothic signatures.

Proverbs 13:20 **"He that walketh with wise men shall be wise: but a companion of fools shall be destroyed."** If our associations don't empower us, enable us, or launch us toward destiny, then it is a useless relationship. If you walk with wise people, you will gain wisdom and eventually be wise. A companion of a wild, foolish, negative, cynical, weak person will eventually succumb and become likeminded. Your associations actually reveal something about whom you are now and where you are going. Whom are you associating with?

5. STAY IN THE PRESENCE OF GOD THROUGH PRAYER, PRAISE, AND WORSHIP WHICH ARE ALL IMPORTANT IN CREATING AN ATMOSPHERE FILLED WITH GOD'S PRESENCE. *John 4:24* **"God is a Spirit: and they that worship him must worship him in spirit and in truth."** *Jude 1:20* **"But ye, beloved, building up yourselves on your most holy faith, praying in the Holy Ghost."** Worship and prayer puts us in the presence of God and in communication spiritually with Him. His presence builds us higher and higher like an edifice. God's presence is filled with love, joy, power, inspiration, revelation, illumination, manifestation, liberation, and so many other wonderful things. *Psalms 16:11* **"Thou wilt show me the path of life: in thy presence is fullness of joy; at thy right hand there are pleasures for evermore."** *2 Corinthians 3:17* **"Now the Lord is that Spirit: and where the Spirit of the Lord is, there is liberty."**

6. HAVE FAITH IN GOD'S WORD IN ORDER TO EMPOWER YOUR FAITH. *Mark 11:22* **"And Jesus answering saith unto them, Have faith in God."** You must have faith *(pistis)* a conviction of religious truth about God. You must be convinced and place that conviction in God. Your inner convincing creates a conviction about God that enables you to embrace Him and whatever He says and does. You are then ready to believe His Word and see your faith

increase. ***Romans 10:17* "So then faith cometh by hearing, and hearing by the word of God."** There is a connection between knowledge and faith. Faith *(pistis)* comes by hearing the Word of God. You must hear the Word of God to have faith and you must have faith when you hear God's Word.

7. EMBRACE YOUR PLACE IN GOD. In order for you to fully appreciate faith and exercise it, you must have some understanding of your true identity. ***Philippians 3:20* "For our conversation is in heaven; from whence also we look for the Saviour, the Lord Jesus Christ."** The word "conversation" comes from the Greek word *politeuma* which means community or citizenship. If you are a child of God, your real citizenship and community is in Heaven. Believers are actually citizens of a Kingdom. It is a country (Hebrews 11:16) that has a King, Jehovah-God, Who rules and reigns. The Kingdom doesn't just exist in a distant place light years from earth. Actually the Kingdom is present within every believer. ***Luke 17:21* "Neither shall they say, Lo here! or, lo there! for, behold, the kingdom of God is within you."**

At the new birth as God entered into our spirit, He brought along the Kingdom and His power with Him. (John 3:3-5; John 14:17; Romans 8:9-11; Ephesians 3:20) You are royalty. He made you heir and joint heir with Christ and you sit in Heavenly places with Christ Jesus. (Romans 8:17; Galatians 4:7; Ephesians 1:3; Ephesians 2:6) You are co-owner of this planet and your Father owns everything. When you embrace your place, you are empowered to live from a position of strength and power not pessimism, apathy, and weakness. The realization of who God has ordained you to be should embolden your position and faith in life. You must accept who you are in God!!

8. USE YOUR FAITH IN ORDER TO EXERCISE AND STRENGTHEN THE MUSCLES OF FAITH. We must realize that faith isn't something we harbor in the spirit or renewed mind, but it must be exercised. We must do some-

thing with the Word of God and faith. *(James 1:22)* Faith produces action or works. *James 2:17-18* **"Even so faith, if it hath not works, is dead, being alone. Yea, a man may say, Thou hast faith, and I have works: show me thy faith without thy works, and I will show thee my faith by my works."** Faith, without works or actions, is dead. The real defining of our faith is by what we do. It isn't enough to just read and say it. You must release it through action. The more you use faith and get good, positive results, the stronger your faith will become.

9. DON'T OVERRATE YOUR FAITH BY TRYING TO DO WHAT YOU SEE PEOPLE WITH GREAT FAITH DO. *Romans 12:3* **"For I say, through the grace given unto me, to every man that is among you, not to think of himself more highly than he ought to think; but to think soberly, according as God hath dealt to every man the measure of faith."** We must be careful that in our quest to strengthen our faith we don't attempt something just because someone else did. I believe there is a law of faith and that law produces results every time. Please remember that when it comes to faith, everyone has it but not in the same measure or quantity. The Bible speaks of variations in quantities of faith from little to great.

People with great faith have usually endured a process that has allowed them to mature to the place spiritually where they embrace God in a deeper dimension. One must be careful that the inspiration of great faith walkers doesn't compel them to attempt to exercise a level of faith that they don't possess. Trying to utilize a dimension of faith that you don't possess could be embarrassing and even disastrous. The seven sons of Sceva learned the hard way that you don't just try something because you see someone else do it. *Acts 19:13-16* **"Then certain of the vagabond Jews, exorcists, took upon them to call over them which had evil spirits the name of the Lord Jesus, saying, We adjure you by Jesus whom Paul preacheth. And there were seven sons**

WHY FAITH? *"Your Guide to Surviving and Thriving in Tough Times"*

of one Sceva, a Jew, and chief of the priests, which did so. And the evil spirit answered and said, Jesus I know, and Paul I know; but who are ye? And the man in whom the evil spirit was leaped on them, and overcame them, and prevailed against them, so that they fled out of that house naked and wounded."

Not only did they not have a relationship with Jesus Christ, but they didn't have the faith, authority, or power to dominate evil spirits. They were whipped, wounded, and stripped of their clothes by the evil spirit and driven out of the house in their birthday suits. Exercise humility in your walk with God. Be patient and let God help you cultivate and nurture your faith. You will know when it is time to actually release faith within the realm of God's will for your life.

10. LEARN FROM YOUR PAST MISTAKES IN ATTEMPTING TO UTILIZE FAITH. This will help perfect your future use of faith. If at first you don't succeed, keep trying. ***Proverbs 16:24a* "For a just man falleth seven times, and riseth up again..."** When we fail in our walk with God, we don't just quit. You must resolve within yourself that sometimes you will fail and fall; but quitting isn't an option. You are an heir who possesses greatness and just because you failed or made an error it doesn't disqualify you from your destiny. Righteous people have failed and will continue to until Jesus returns. But they don't stay down. They keep getting up. It is true that sometimes we failed in utilizing faith for money, ministry, jobs, relationships, healing, miracles, and so much more.

There are times we have asked or tried to exercise faith for the wrong reasons. ***James 4:3*** says, **"Ye ask, and receive not, because ye ask amiss, that ye may consume it upon your lusts."** Sometimes it is our lifestyle that isn't pleasing to God. ***James 4:4*** says, **"Ye adulterers and adulteresses, know ye not that the friendship of the world is enmity with God? whosoever therefore will be a friend of the world is the enemy of God."** Do your best to make sure that your life lines up with God's expectations within His Word. You don't have to worry about being perfect. Just strive with humility to live a good life with the help of the Holy Spirit and you will be covered by His grace. ***James 4:6* "But he giveth more grace. Wherefore he saith, God resisteth the proud, but giveth grace unto the humble."**

I don't know any baby who attempted to walk that never stumbled or fell. Truthfully you will stumble and fall but don't quit. GET UP BECAUSE GOD HAS YOU COVERED AND HIS GRACE HAS GIVEN YOU FAVOR!!

A PRAYER OF REPENTANCE

If you have come this far with me in the journey of reading "Why Faith?" and you don't know Jesus Christ as your Lord and savior; I want to take the time to encourage you to submit your life to Him. The best thing you could ever do is leave your old, past, sinful life behind and embrace a new life with Jesus Christ. You don't have to know and understand everything about God but you do have to have faith that He loves you and will secure your life eternally. Take a leap of faith; I will stand with you before God now. Let's start something fresh and new today.

Say this prayer with me now: *"Dear Jehovah-God I have sinned against you and I am sorry. I believe in my heart that Jesus is your son who died on the cross for my sins. I have made a decision to ask Jesus Christ into my heart as Lord and Savior. Please Jesus come into my life; forgive me of all my sins. I need your love and your grace. Jesus I receive you into my heart and embrace you now as my Lord and Savior. I am now a new creature, old things have moved out of my life and all things are brand new. I am born again. I happily and boldly declare that I am saved and Jesus is Lord. This I pray in the wonderful name of Jesus Christ. Amen"*

Congratulations if you said that prayer sincerely from your heart you have met the requirements of Romans 10:9-10 and are now a part of God's family. May God Bless and keep you.

WORKS CITED

Agency for Healthcare Research and Quality. <u>National Healthcare Quality Report,2003</u>. 7 Nov. 2008 <u>http://www.ahrq.gov/qual/nhqr03/nhqr03.htm</u>.

Lastoria, M. D. "Depression." <u>Baker Encyclopedia of Psychology & Counseling</u>. Eds. David G. Benner and Peter C. Hill. 2nd ed. Grand Rapids: Baker Books, 1999.

Murray PhD, Bob and Alicia Fortinberry MS. "Depression Facts and Stats." <u>Uplift Program</u>. 15 Jan. 2005. 7 Nov. 2008 <u>http://www.upliftprogram.com/depression_stats.html#3</u>.

"The Numbers Count: Mental Disorders in America." <u>National Institute of Mental Health</u>. 26 June 2008. 7 Nov. 2008 <u>http://www.nimh.nih.gov/health/publications/the-numbers-count-mental-disorders-in-america.shtml</u>.

For more information on sermons and other materials
By Dr. A. G. Green

Visit Dr. Green on the World Wide Web

www.aggreenministries.org

Printed in the United States
136778LV00003B/7/P